For the Hero of World War II

Liberty Bell Publications
2004

First Published 1989 by
Liberty Bell Publications
Reedy, WV USA

Reprinted 2004 by
Liberty Bell Publications
PO Box 890
York, SC 29745
www.libertybellpublications.com
803.684.4408

ISBN: 1-59364-013-7

TABLE OF CONTENTS

In Remembrance of
Adolf Hitler's 100th Birthday
20 April 1989

Zum 20. April 1989

Vergangen—
aber nicht
vergessen—
Du lebst in
unseren Herzen!

Aus deinem Bild,   Der unverletzt
Aus deinem Gesicht   Den Weg uns weist
Ein Glaube quillt,   Und Berge versetzt
Ein Wille spricht,   Und Deutschland heißt.

20 April 1889   **20 April 1989 — 1**   *30 April 1945*

Die Saga vom Dritten Reich

Ich, einer von den Alten, die noch leben,
Will mich aus diesem Schmutz der Zeit erheben
Und künden, was ein Leben lang uns trieb
Und dessen Abglanz meinem Herzen blieb.

Ein Meer von Schlamm erstickte Glanz und Licht.
Verrat und Lüge hatten mehr Gewicht,
Mit rohen Kräften einer Welt gepaart,
Die nie des edlen Wollens inne ward,
Dem wir gehorchten, unverzagt und treu.
Mein letzter Stolz bleibt: ich war auch dabei.

O hehres Losungswort: ein Volk, ein Reich,
Ein Führer — und ein Schwert mit gutem Streich —
Und eine Fahne schwarz und weiß und rot
Mit einer Rune, die dem Übel droht —
Der Traum der Väter — endlich Wirklichkeit —
Acht Jahre lang — o unvergeßne Zeit —
Was sind die Schatten schon an deinem Licht.
Verlogne Welt, der es an Glanz gebricht —
Sie maß den Adel nur mit der Gewalt
Und nahm uns Ehre, Sitte und Gestalt
Bewußt und haßerfüllt, und gab dafür
Uns ihren Abschaum: Sklavensinn und Gier —
Und eine Meute von gekauften Knechten,
Die ihre Wut am eignen Blute rächten.

Acht Jahre — hoffnungsvoller Anbeginn —
Glückhaft ein jeder Tag und voll Gewinn.
Der Deutsche, überdrüssig hohler Worte,
Packt wieder zu und wirkt an seinem Orte.
Er schaut den andern mutig ins Gesicht
Und fordert sich sein Recht und seine Pflicht.

20 April 1889   **20 April 1989 – 2**   *30 April 1945*

Die Achtung steigt, das Schwert wächst in der Hand.
Im Morgenglanze steht das Vaterland,
Die Künste blühn — es füllen sich die Wiegen —
Sie zeugen heut noch wider tausend Lügen.
Ein frohes Volk schart sich um seine Fahnen,
Erlöst und frei und würdig seiner Ahnen.
Was sind die Schatten schon an jenen Tagen —
Für jedes Volk in Freiheit leicht zu tragen.

Die kleine Schar der Lumpen schwieg gelähmt.
Der offne Gegner wurde bald beschämt
Und kehrte still ins Vaterhaus zurück,
Und Tage kamen voller Glanz und Glück.
Ein Volk — ein Reich — klang es durch deutsche Lande.
O Österreich, es fielen deine Bande!

Vom Nordseestrande bis zum Memelstrom,
Vom Böhmerwalde bis zum Stefansdom
Erschollen wieder frei die alten Lieder,
Und namenloses Glück ergriff die Brüder,
Die eben noch ein fremdes Joch ertrugen,
Die Glocken klangen und die Herzen schlugen.
Ein Volk — ein Reich — o unvergeßne Stunden —
Gedenk ich euer, bluten tausend Wunden.

Der Haß der Feinde wuchs ins Grenzenlose.
Das Schicksal mischte seine dunklen Lose.
Erstanden war der Bau in Herrlichkeit.
Doch in den Gründen wühlten Lug und Neid,
Vernichtung wollten sie und Acht und Bann.
Und dieses Wissen trug der große Mann
Mit schwerem Herzen durch die langen Nächte.
Er rang mit seinem Gotte um das Rechte.
Er sah das Ende des Aones nahen,
Indes die Schurken nur den Gegner sahen:
Das Deutsche Reich — ihm galt ihr Haßgeschrei.
Da schlug ein Gott den Menschenwahn entzwei.

Und kühne Siege zierten Deutschlands Farben
Und Helden, zahllos, seinem Ruhme starben.
Doch unwert war Europa dieser Größe.
Es sah voll Haß des Heiligen Reiches Blöße.
Die Rachsucht ließ ihm Rast nicht und nicht Ruh.
Sie stieß verblendet mit dem Dolche zu.

Da ward das Schicksal des Äons besiegelt.
Die letzte Rettungspforte stand verriegelt,
Und unter irrem Haß- und Sieggeschrei
Brach das Gefüge dieser Zeit entzwei.

Haß, Wahn und Lüge und die blinde Gier:
Nun ist die Schreckensherrschaft dieser vier,
Zerstückelt und geschändet liegt das Reich —
Und donnernd ruft die Rache: wehe euch!
Euch wird sie bald das gleiche Schicksal geben.

Wenn Deutschland fällt, dann soll die Erde beben.

1930 · 1937

20 April 1889   20 April 1989 — 4   30 April 1945

The Measure of Greatness

by William L. Pierce

April 20 of this year is the 100th anniversary of the birth of the greatest man of our era—a man who dared more and achieved more, who set his aim higher and climbed higher, who felt more deeply and stirred the souls of those around him more mightily, who was more closely attuned to the Life Force which permeates our cosmos and gives it meaning and purpose, and did more to serve that Life Force, than any other man of our times.

And yet he is the most reviled and hated man of our times. Only a few tens of thousands of men and women, in scattered groups around the world, will celebrate his birthday with love and reverence on April 20, while all of the scribblers and commentators of the controlled news media, the controlled politicians, and the controlled churchmen will pour out their hatred and venom and lies against him, and those lies will be believed by hundreds of millions.

What is the measure of greatness in a man?

Only the most vulgar and doctrinaire democrat would seriously equate greatness with popularity—although in any polling of average citizens on their choice for the greatest man of the century there are certain to be substantial numbers of votes for Elvis Presley, John Kennedy, Billy Graham, Michael Jackson, and various other high-visibility lightweights: charismatic entertainers on the stage of politics, rock concerts, spectator sports, or what have you.

More serious citizens would pass by the lightweights and choose men who have changed the world in some way. We would hear choices like Franklin Roosevelt ("he saved the world from fascism"), Albert Einstein ("he taught us about the nature of our universe"), and Martin Luther King ("he helped us achieve racial justice"), depending upon whether one's personal inclinations lay more in the direction of politics, science, or racial self-abasement, respectively.

But if the poll asked instead for the most evil man of the century, or the most hated man, or the man having the most negative influence, at least three-quarters of the blue-collar and the white-collar pollees alike would name one man: Adolf Hitler. This, however, would be merely a reflection of the role assigned to him by the controlled mass media, rather than a truly informed and reasoned choice.

All of this raises several very interesting issues. There is, for example, the question of how we came to the preposterous state of affairs prevailing today, wherein we place the destiny of our nation, our planet, and our race in the hands of a mass of voters whose powers of judgment are manifested in such things as the type of television entertainment their preferences have pushed into prime time and the type of men they have elected to public office. And there is the equally weighty question of how, knowing the ease with which this mass is misled, we permitted virtually all of the media of mass information and entertainment to fall into the hands of a race whose interests are so diametrically opposed to our own.

Perhaps even more pertinent to a consideration of human greatness, however, is the question of how our system of values came to be turned on its head, so that Franklin Roosevelt is regarded as a hero and Adolf Hitler as a villain, not only by the stolid and stunned masses, but also by a majority of the supposedly "educated" elite, many of whom pride themselves on their intellectual independence.

Whether we judge the greatness of a man by his intrinsic

qualities of character and soul or by his accomplishments, Adolf Hitler had greatness of a very high order – if we use the standards which have been traditional in our race.

We cannot, of course, make comparisons with all the "mute, inglorious Miltons" whose lack of notable accomplishment has made them anonymous, despite the sterling inner qualities they may have possessed. But when Hitler's character is held up beside those of other 20th-century political leaders, he stands as a giant among pygmies.

At the prosaic level, we can note his ascetic personal habits, compared with Winston Churchill's habitual drunkenness and notorious self-indulgence; or his personal loyalty to those who had been his comrades in the days of political struggle, compared with Joseph Stalin's habit of murdering his former comrades by the dozen, as potential rivals, as soon as he no longer needed their services; or his direct, frank, and straightforward manner, compared to the cunning deviousness which was Franklin Roosevelt's trademark.

At the spiritual level, the inner differences between Hitler and his contemporaries are even more striking. Hitler was a man with a mission, from the beginning. The testimony of his closest associates, from his boyhood days to the end of his life, agrees with the observations of more distant and impartial observers: Hitler had a mystical sense of destiny, a sense of having been singled out and called by a higher power to devote his life to the service of his race.

His childhood companion August Kubizek has related extraordinary evidence of this when Hitler was only 16 years old.[1] Twenty years later, while he was in prison after an unsuccessful attempt to overthrow the government, Hitler himself wrote of his motivation in a way which suggested the range of his vision:

> What we must fight for is the security of the existence and reproduction of our race and our people, the sustenance of our children and the maintenance of the purity of our blood . . . so that our people may mature for

1. August Kubizek, *Adolf Hitler, mein Jugendfreund* (Graz, 1953), pp. 127-135.

the fulfillment of the mission allotted them by the Creator of the universe.

Every thought and every idea, every doctrine and all knowledge, must serve this purpose. And everything must be examined from this point of view and used or rejected according to its utility. Then no theory will stiffen into a dead doctrine, since it is life alone that all things must serve. . . .

. . . [T]he National Socialist philosophy finds the importance of mankind in its basic racial elements. In the state it sees on principle a means to an end and construes that end as the preservation of the racial existence of man. . . .

And so the National Socialist philosophy of life corresponds to the innermost will of Nature, since it restores that free play of forces which must lead to a continuous mutual higher breeding, until finally the best of humanity, having achieved possession of this earth, will have a free play for activity in domains which will lie partly above it and partly outside it.

We all sense that in the distant future humanity must be faced by problems which only a highest race, become master people and supported by the means and possibilities of an entire globe, will be equipped to overcome. . . .

Thus, the highest purpose of a National Socialist state is concern for the preservation of those original racial elements which bestow culture and create the beauty and dignity of a higher mankind. We, as Aryans, can conceive of the state only as the living organism of a nationality which not only assures the preservation of this nationality, but by the development of its spiritual and ideal abilities leads it to the highest freedom. . . .

A National Socialist state must begin by raising marriage from the level of a continuous defilement of the race and give it the consecration of an institution which is called upon to produce images of the Lord and not monstrosities halfway between man and ape. . . .

It must set race in the center of all life. It must take care to keep it pure. It must declare the child to be the most precious treasure of the people. It must see to it that only the healthy beget children . . . .

The National Socialist state must make certain that by a suitable education of youth it will someday obtain a race ripe for the last and greatest decisions on this earth. . . .

. . .[A]nyone who wants to cure this era, which is inwardly sick and rotten, must first summon the courage to make clear the causes of this disease. And this should be the concern of the National Socialist movement: pushing aside all narrowmindedness, to gather and to organize from the ranks of our nation those forces capable of becoming the vanguard fighters for a new philosophy of life. . . .

We are not simple enough to believe that it could ever be possible to bring about a perfect era. But this relieves no one of the obligation to combat recognized errors, to overcome weaknesses, and to strive for the ideal. Harsh reality of its own accord will create only too many limitations. For that very reason, however, man must try to serve the ultimate goal, and failures must not deter him, any more than he can abandon a system of justice because mistakes creep into it, or any more than medicine is discarded because there always will be sickness in spite of it.

> We National Socialists know that with this conception we stand as revolutionaries in the world of today and are branded as such. But our thoughts and actions must in no way be determined by the approval or disapproval of our time, but by the binding obligation to a truth which we have recognized.[2]

Hitler's opponents, Churchill and Roosevelt, were party politicians, with the minds and souls of party politicians. Great, impersonal goals, just as truth, meant nothing at all to them. The only thing that counted was the approval or disapproval of their times: the outcome of the next election, a good press claque, votes. Only Stalin shared in any way Hitler's disdain for approval; only Stalin was motivated to any degree by an impersonal idea. But the idea that Stalin served was the alien, destructive idea of Jewish Marxism. And while Hitler served the Life Force with the instincts of a seer, Stalin served Marxism with the instincts of a bureaucrat and a butcher.

A comparison of careers leads us to a similar ranking of greatness of soul. Churchill and Roosevelt were born into the political establishment. They fed at the public trough for years, in one office after another, grabbing greedily at opportunities for a bigger serving of swill. But it was circumstance, not their own efforts, which thrust them onto the stage of world history.

Stalin hacked out his own niche in history to a much greater extent than his western allies, and he was an incomparably stronger man than either of them. He was tough, ruthless, infinitely cunning, and utterly determined to prevail, no matter what the obstacles. Even so, his struggle for prominence and power was entirely within the Bolshevik party and its predecessors. He was the consummate bureaucratic infighter, not the innovator or the lone pioneer.

2. Adolf Hitler, *Mein Kampf*

Only Adolf Hitler started literally from nothing and through the exercise of a superhuman will created the physical basis for the realization of his vision. In 1918, recovering from a British poison-gas attack in a veterans' hospital, he made the decision to enter politics in order to serve that vision. He was a 29-year-old invalid, with no money, no family, no friends or connections, no university education, and no experience. Liberals, Jews, and communists ruled his country, making him and all those to whom he might appeal for support outsiders.

Five and one-half years later he was sentenced to five years in prison for his political activity, and his enemies thought that was the end of him and his movement. But less than nine years after being sentenced he was Chancellor of Germany, with the strongest and most progressive nation in Europe at his command. He had built the National Socialist movement and led it to victory over the organized opposition of the entire Establishment: conservatives, liberals, communists, Jews, and Christians.

He then transformed Germany, lifting it out of its economic depression (while Americans, under Roosevelt, continued to line up at the soup kitchens), restoring its spirit (and much of the territory which had been taken from it by the victors of the First World War), stimulating its artistic and scientific creativity, and winning the admiration (or, in some cases, the envy and hatred) of other nations. It was an achievement hardly paralleled in the history of the world. Even those who do not understand the real significance of his creation must concede that.

And what was the *real* significance of Hitler's work? One of his most earnest admirers in India, Savitri Devi, has given us a poetic answer to that question. She wrote:

> . . . [I]n its essence, the National Socialist idea exceeds not only Germany and our times, but the Aryan race and mankind itself and any epoch; . . . it ultimately expresses that mysterious and unfailing wisdom according to which Nature lives and creates: the impersonal wisdom of the primeval forest and of the ocean depth and of the spheres in the dark fields of space; and . . . it is Adolf Hitler's glory not merely to have gone back to that divine wisdom — stigmatizing man's silly infatuation for "intellect," his child-

ish pride in "progress," and his criminal attempt to enslave Nature—but to have made it the basis of a practical regeneration policy of worldwide scope, precisely now, in our overcrowded, overcivilized, and technically overevolved world, at the very end of the dark age.[3]

More prosaically, Hitler's work, in contrast to that of his contemporaries, was *above* politics, *above* economics, *above* nationalism. He had mobilized a powerful, modern state and placed it at the service of our race, so that our race might become fit to serve as an agent of the Life Force.

Perceptive and idealistic young men from every nation in Europe—and from many nations outside Europe as well—recognized this significance, and they flocked to serve him and to fight for his cause, even at the cost of censure and ostracism from their more parochial and narrowminded countrymen. There was never before an elite fighting force to match the *SS*, which by the end of the Second World War had more non-Germans than Germans in it.

The war, of course, is counted as Hitler's great failure, even as the proof of his lack of greatness, by his detractors. It merely proves that he was a man, not a god, even if a divine will worked through him, and that he could not perform miracles. He could not defend himself forever, with the governments of nearly the whole world allied in a total war to pull him down and destroy his creation, so that they and the interests they served could return to "business as usual." Even so, he gave a far better account of himself than any of his adversaries.

And what will count in the long run in determining Adolf Hitler's stature is not whether he lost or won the war, but whether it was he or his adversaries who were on the side of the Life Force, whether it was he or they who served the cause of Truth and human progress. We only have to look around us today to know it was not they.   □

Reprinted with permission from *National Vanguard*, No. 110, March-April 1989.   Subscriptions $12.00 for six issues, available from National Vanguard Books, POB 330, Hillsboro WV 24946

Der Führer

50 Jahre für Deutschlands Ewigkeit

Die Stunde kam, da er sein Werk erkannte,
Jäh stand er auf, zum Opfergang bereit.
Und mit dem Feuer seiner Rede brannte
Er seine Flammen in die Dunkelheit.

Erschüttert lauschten die in Scham Entbrannten,
Der Kreis der Sehnsucht rundete zur Tat,
Und jubelnd folgten sie dem Gott-Gesandten,
Die dumpfe Menge aber schrie Verrat.

Schwer war sein Weg . . der Schande Ketten klirrten,
An Deutschlands Herzen fraß der fremde Tod;
Doch endlich hörten die in Wahn Verirrten,
Sie sahen ihn und sahen ihre Not.

So kam sein Tag . . Millionen Herzen wandten
Sich hin zu ihm und wußten ihre Pflicht.
Der Nebel fiel. Die Morgenfeuer brannten,
Groß stand er da . . . und um ihn stand das Licht.

Fritz Wolke

HIS IDEA LIVES!

HIS LEGACY   OUR OBLIGATION!

20 April 1889   20 April 1989 — 13   *30 April 1945*

April 1937
IV. Jahrg. · 4. Folge

Der Schulungsbrief

Das zentrale Monatsblatt der NSDAP. und DAF. (Hauptschulungsamt der NSDAP. und Schulungsamt der DAF.) Herausgeber: Der Reichsorganisationsleiter

Ich bin ein Deutscher. Ich glaube an mein Volk. Ich glaube an seine Ehre. Ich glaube an seine Zukunft. Ich glaube an sein Recht, und ich trete ein für dieses Recht. Ich trete ein für seine Freiheit, und ich trete damit ein für einen besseren Frieden, als den Frieden des Unsegens und des Hasses der Vergangenheit. Das glaube ich, und das bekenne ich im Namen meines Volkes vor der ganzen Welt.   Adolf Hitler

20 April 1889   *20 April 1989 – 14*   *30 April 1945*

AN AMERICAN VETERAN'S REFLECTIONS ON THE SIGNIFICANCE OF THE LIFE OF ADOLF HITLER

by
Charles E. Weber

On 20 April commemorative celebrations of Adolf Hitler's 100th birthday will have taken place in many parts of the world, probably many more outside Germany than within it, as anomalous that might seem.

Why does the world continue to be fascinated by Hitler nearly a half century after his government was utterly defeated in one of the most costly and tragic wars in the history of mankind, perhaps even more devastating to Germany in particular than the Thirty Year War (1618-1648)? During the Second World War Germany lost at least a quarter of its territory. Nearly four million German civilians and three million German men in military service perished. Since 1945 Germany has been governed by politicians whose status has been little better than officials chosen by occupying powers.

Today, Aryan nations are psychologically divided and are in a state of decline and retreat, with prospects which are by no means encouraging to them. "The Passing of the Great Race" now has a far more ominous sound than when it was used by Madison Grant over seven decades ago as the title of a book which still has significance for us (see *Instauration*, January 1989, page 11). Even in the USSR, Russians are painfully aware of their declining numbers in relation to other ethnic components of the USSR. Portugal, the last truly colonial power, gave up Angola and Mozambique as long ago as 1975. The British, French and Dutch empires had become mere shadows long before that. Aryans loyal to their race have looked with horror at the loss of Rhodesia and the nasty threats against the Caucasian component of South Africa, where the Negro has the highest standard of living in all of Africa. American politicians indifferent to the future of Aryan nations or even hostile toward them join in these threats with a cynicism that defies the imagination. (For reasons for this decline of the Aryan nations, see *Bulletin* 19, "The Continuing Psychological Burdens Imposed on Aryan Americans by the Second World War," republished in the *Liberty Bell* of January 1987.) Racial conflict in England is common enough but it is of only modest importance compared to racial conflict (including racially motivated crime against Aryans) in the United States, where "inner cities" have become so lawless that Caucasians walk their streets only at the risk of their lives. "Affirmative Action" is a cynical euphemism for the enforcement of economic disadvantages to Aryan Americans. So effete and corrupt have American politicians become that they turned over one of the greatest engineering feats of Aryan man, the magnificent canal at Panama, to a Marxist government of a country largely populated by non-Aryans, for whom such an undertaking would have been out of the question.

If, in the year 1989, we see swastikas painted on walls in many places, we must ascribe that to the nagging fears of the Aryan men who think independently enough to be proud of their racial heritage, inspite of the brainwashing of schools and media, and to the image of Adolf Hitler as a man who was truly dedicated to the welfare of his people, a man who died by his own hand rather than surrendering during the stubborn defense of the badly battered capital of the Reich in 1945.

It has been observed that a swastika on the cover of a book practically guarantees its commercial success in the United States, even if that book is full of the most absurd fiction intended to denigrate National Socialism. All over the United States, especially in western states, large gun shows are held in which prized and historically interesting firearms and war memorabilia are displayed, exchanged and sold. Amongst the memorabilia which characteristically bring high prices — sometimes unbelievably high prices — are German firearms, flags, uniforms and military decorations from the National Socialist period. Why? What accounts for this?

Hitler's most famous writing, the voluminous *Mein Kampf*, was copyrighted in 1925 and 1927, when Hitler was still in his 30's. Even today parts of this work are pertinent reading for Americans. Although *Mein Kampf* is a largely autobiographical work, as its title implies, and is also largely concerned with the results of the Versailles "Treaty" and efforts to overcome its effects, the book reflects a broad range of reading and thought on Hitler's part. On page 479 of the 1943 Eher-Verlag edition Hitler writes favorably about the social mobility he perceived in American society and envisages opportunities for higher education for qualified young Germans of all social strata. This was an American influence on National Socialism in addition to those which we pointed out in *Bulletins* 5 and 19 (republished in the *Liberty Bell* issues of February 1987 and January 1988). Even as early as the years during which Hitler was writing *Mein Kampf* he envisaged an improvement of the quality of human life through *Rassenhygiene* and the sterilization of persons afflicted with incurable diseases (pages 279 and 444-451 of the aforementioned edition). It must be pointed out here that eugenic sterilization had long been established as a principle of law in many American states. In later years Hitler magnanimously donated 100,000 Reichsmark, a huge sum at that time, from his personal financial resources for a campaign against smoking, which he perceived as a serious and costly health hazard in Germany. (See page 240 of R. Proctor's *Racial Hygiene*, Harvard University Press, 1988.) Even Hitler's most intense detractors can hardly deny that he had a large measure of idealistic motivation.

Two years after Hitler assumed power in Germany, in January 1935, the Saar plebiscite took place under the League of Nations, one of the few instances in which Germany regained territory lost after the First World War on the basis of the principle of self-determination promised by President Wilson. Approximately 90% of the voters of the Saar chose to return to Germany, clearly demonstrating the hopes which National Socialism inspired in Germans after a time sufficient to demonstrate its nature. Much the same can be said of the reunion of Austria and Germany in 1938, a desire for which had been expressed in the official name of Austria after 1918, *Deutschösterreich* (see *Bulletin* 6). Even the Time-Life series on the Second World War (*Prelude to War*, 1977, p. 193) described the reception of German forces as follows:

> "When German troops crossed into Austria on Saturday, March 12, they were welcomed with flowers and Nazi flags. Hitler arrived later that day to a rapturous reception in his hometown of Linz. A similar ovation greeted him in Vienna, scene of his dismal young manhood. As his big black Mercedes-Benz traveled the country's roads, adoring onlookers knelt to scoop up bits of earth the car's tires had touched."

In November 1988, Phillip Jenninger, President of the Bundestag, was forced to resign his important position just because part of his speech commemorating the Kristallnacht contained an enumeration of Hitler's astonishing successes during 1933-1938. (See *Bulletin* 33, republished in the *Liberty Bell* of March 1989.)

Although Hitler was clearly popular amongst the masses of the German people, he had his domestic enemies and detractors. This hostility came to its fullest fruition in the desperate days after the successful Allied landings in Normandy. On 20 July 1944 Hitler survived—one might say miraculously—an assassination attempt which had been carefully planned by high-ranking German military officers. As Generalmajor Otto Ernst Remer has pointed out, this group of officers consisted largely of members of the nobility (see *Bulletin* 11, republished in the *Liberty Bell* of June 1987).

In 11 December 1941 Hitler delivered a long speech before the Reichstag in which circumstances finally forced him to recognize that a *de facto* state of war existed for quite some time between the United States and Germany. Hitler placed the responsibility for this state of war squarely on Roosevelt and took the occasion to contrast his own life with Roosevelt's life. Hitler recognized Roosevelt as a man who was exercising his great power in an effort to destroy Germany. It was Roosevelt who was Hitler's most bitter and powerful enemy and who succeeded in involving the United States in a war in which the United States played the decisive rôle in the defeat of Germany (and hence the securing of Communist power throughout the world), although only a quite modest portion of the American people had wanted a direct involvement in the war in Europe.

Let us consider a few revealing paragraphs (in my translation) in which Hitler analyzed the psychological differences between himself and his powerful, cunning personal enemy:

> We know what force stands behind Roosevelt. It is that eternal Jew who believes that his time has come in order to carry out on us that which we all had to see and experience with horror in Soviet Russia. Now we have become acquainted with the Jewish paradise on earth. Millions of German soldiers have been able to gain a personal insight into a country in which this international Jew [cf. the title of the studies on the Jewish question sponsored by Henry Ford during 1920-1922 (*The International Jew: The World's Foremost Problem*, 4 volumes, approx. 1,000 pp., $26.00 + $3.90 for postage and handling, available from Liberty Bell Publications)] destroyed and annihilated human beings and property. The President of the United States can perhaps not grasp that. If so, that is a sign of his intellectual limitations. ....
>
> National Socialism came to power in the same year in which Roosevelt was elected President of the United States. It is now important to examine the factors which must be considered the cause of the present development:
>
> Roosevelt comes from an immensely wealthy [steinreich] family and belonged from the outset to that class of people for whom birth and background pave the path of life in the democracies and thus assure their rise.
>
> As for myself, I was the only child of a small, poor family and had to struggle for my path by work and diligence under unspeakable efforts.
>
> When the [First] World War came about, under Wilson's shadow Roosevelt experienced the war outside the sphere of the wage earner. He knows only the pleasant effects of the quarrels of nations and states which yield advantages for the man who makes profits while other bleed.
>
> At the same time my own life was in a quite different position, on the other hand. I was not among those who made history or even just carried on business transactions, but rather among those who carried out orders.
>
> As an ordinary soldier I tried to do my duty in the face of the enemy during those four years. Naturally, I returned from the war just as poor as I had gone into it in the autumn of 1914. I thus shared my fate with that of millions, while Mr. Franklin Roosevelt shared his fate with that of the so-

called Upper Ten Thousand. While Mr. Roosevelt was trying out his abilities just after the war in financial speculations in order to make personal profits from the inflation, that is, from the misery of others, I was still lying in a military hospital, like many hundreds of thousands of others.

(For translations of other passages from Hitler's speech of 11 December 1941, see *Bulletin* 29, republished in the *Liberty Bell* of November 1988.)

After the war the Allied occupation forces did their best to efface and denigrate the memory of Hitler. It was even forbidden to sell postage stamps with the portrait of Hitler to collectors. The effort to denigrate the memory of Hitler has continued with such energy since 1945 that one must suspect that the denigrators have a real fear that Hitler's ideas and personality still have a great potential which must be suppressed by any means, fair or foul. The greatest recent living symbol of National Socialism, Rudolf Hess, whose peace mission in 1941 could have prevented untold suffering, had to be kept incarcerated to the end of his days and there is important evidence that Hess was, in fact, murdered.

The methodical, shrewd and persistent denigration, in schools and media, of Hitler and everything for which he stood, even that which was inspired by American thinking, has caused an irrational and chaotic approach to many problems, not only in Germany itself, but in nations which were the putative victors in the Second World War (see *Bulletin* 19). In a series of astute observations a physician, Dr. Siegfried Ernst, described this psychological chaos in an article under the title, "Wegen Hitler keine Rettung aus dem Chaos?" (No rescue from the Chaos Because of Hitler?). The article was republished in the 20 September 1986 issue of *Eidgenoss* [an excellent and highly-recommended German-language monthly published by the astute Dr. Max Wahl], CH-8401 Winterthur, Switzerland. Dr. Ernst's observations are formulated in a pattern, of which we shall give four examples in translation out of his 32:

> Since Hitler publicized the motto, "Gemeinnutz geht vor Eigennutz" (the welfare of the community takes precedence over the welfare of the individual), today the welfare of the individual must always come before the welfare of the community. [Note: this motto was on the edge of the 5

Reichsmark silver piece struck in 900/1000 silver during 1934-1939.]

Since Hitler gave decorations to mothers who bore large families [Mutterkreuze], the women of today are supposed to have as few children as possible.

Since Hitler combatted homosexuality, it must therefore be openly advocated today.

Since Hitler introduced the Reichsarbeitsdienst [National Labor Service], to overcome unemployment and class consciousness, today no service can be required any longer from the unemployed for the community.

There can hardly be any question that the relative general welfare of the Aryan component of the U.S. population is deteriorating. Its birthrate is catastrophic and measures against that component, such as the graduated income tax, and slaps in the face, such as "Affirmative Action" (see the Exxon Corporation publication *The Lamp*, Fall 1988, pp. 18-19 as a particularly vexing example), are eventually going to cause the Aryan component to become aware of its plight and those resspansible for it. The emotional reaction could gather force like an avalanche. Since Hitler could become a symbol of loyalty and devotion to the Aryan nations, there is almost certainly going to be a more favorable evaluation of the meaning of Adolf Hitler's life as ever more Aryans become aware of their plight in the United States.

Finally, let us mention two recent books which give interesting insights into Hitler's personality and life:

Hans Baur, *Hitler at my Side* [$22.50 + $3.50 for postage and handling, available from Liberty Bell Publications], Houston, 1986. (Baur was Hitler's personal air pilot.)

Billy F. Price (editor), *Adolf Hitler als Maler und Zeichner* (Adolf Hitler as a Painter and Drawer), Zug, 1983. (Contains magnificent reproductions of Hitler's artistic efforts.) [Also available: VHS video cassette *Adolf Hitler: Artist-Architect-Designer*, $50. from Liberty Bell Publications.]

HITLER AT 100:

A CRITICAL ASSESSMENT

by Hans Schmidt

One hundred years from now, just about this time of the year, journalists all over the world will be delving into yellowed archives to find out what our generation had written on the occasion of the 100th anniversary of the birth of Adolf Hitler on 20 April 1989. No doubt they will be amazed at what they discover was said about the man whom they will probably regard as the most important personality of the Twentieth Century. Either there will be no mention of him, or he will be ridiculed, or else he will be depicted as the devil incarnate of our era.

Forty-four years after Adolf Hitler's suicide in the bunker underneath the Reich Chancellory at Berlin, it is still very difficult to write an objective review on the German Führer, even though there are currently more books and articles on his life in print than on any of his major adversaries. Thankfully, the judgment of history does not depend on the emotions of a man's contemporaries. Attempts to bestow the designation "the Great" on a mediocre ruler while he still lives are usually as futile as, conversely, were the relatively recent efforts by the East German Communists to take this honorary title away from Frederick the Great, one of the truly great

Prussian Kings. Hitler knew this, and he was convinced that—when all is said, and centuries in the future—he considered his mission would be regarded with more fairness and objectivity than now.

Already we know that we can neither view nor judge the German World War II leader by the same standards we use in regard to his greatest adversaries, namely Franklin Delano Roosevelt, Winston Churchill, and Joseph Stalin. Ironically, the world press contributes greatly to this state of affairs by glibly excusing the obvious war crimes of the Allied leaders, no matter how horrible they were, and ascribing some sort of odd singularity to the Führer's real or imagined transgressions. This alleged uniqueness of Hitler's actions may in the future contribute toward the creation of a myth surrounding his person that cannot be found in connection with any of the other three men mentioned above. In the United States Roosevelt is all but forgotten. Stalin still has many adherents in the Soviet Union, but the most recent revelations about his crimes will make certain that, henceforth, it will be ever more difficult to defend him and his actions. Churchill's reputation rests largely on the self-promoting books he has written, and on the fact that the British establishment, as a matter of self-interest, is very much intent upon defending his conduct before and during the war. However, books such as David Irving's *Churchill's War* will no doubt cause more people to view Churchill's life with skepticism, and one can safely assume that future historians will be less kind to him than are many of his still living admirers.

It is a pity that so many writers and commentators of the present use old and untenable clichés when writing of Hitler and Germany. It is as if they fear to acknowledge the incongruity of some of their own statements. Here are some:

1. Hitler wanted to conquer the world.

2. Hitler intended to invade the United States.

3. Hitler started World War II.

4. Hitler was against Christianity.

5. It was Hitler's plan to annihilate the Jews (and he had said so

in his book *Mein Kampf*).

To point No. 1, one can only say that many Germans still wish "der Adolf" had set his aim higher than merely creating a Greater Germany and seeking German hegemony over Europe. Had he planned for world conquest, he might have won. There is the old adage, "the higher the mountain one intends to climb, the higher one gets in reality." Certainly, Hitler with his limited European ambitions had little chance to win a *world* war against at least *four* major adversaries (USA, USSR, Great Britain, and World Jewry) who were used to thinking and fighting in global power terms. WW II Germany's position vis-à-vis those four major powers was like that of an Olympic fencer abiding by sportsmen's rules who is opposing a professional military swordsman out for a kill. Even in 1940 One could not conquer the world, or invade the United States (point No. 2), with 750 ton U-Boats, 200-km range "Stukas" and little tanks with short barrel guns, *and* without either a strategic Navy or Air Force. Hitler's soldiers often accomplished the nearly impossible, but it is doubtful even they could have crossed the Atlantic on "split-in-half" Rhine barges (such as were prepared for the planned invasion of England after the British had rejected the German peace overtures).

3. Did Hitler really start World War II? Even the question sounds incongruous, doesn't it? There is no doubt that the German *Wehrmacht* under Hitler's command invaded Poland on 1 September 1939, and that this action escalated into World War II. However, if an American President assumes the right to invade a country (Grenada) a thousand miles from the US border because the lives of a few American citizen *might* be threatened, certainly Hitler had the right to come to the defense of a million Germans who at that time were mistreated, *and many of whom were murdered*, on former German territory right next door to the Reich. It was the phony British guarantee for Poland which created a world war out of a local European conflict. Had the guarantee been legitimate, then Great Britain would also have declared war on the Soviet Union when it invaded Poland 17 days afterward, and London would not have abandoned Poland after 1945.

---

4. There is no question that Adolf Hitler regarded the Christian religion as a major and fundamental force of Western Civilization. No *official* attempt was made to wean the German people from it. It bears mentioning that the German armed forces, including units of the Waffen-SS, had chaplains throughout the war (and attendance at church services was never hindered), whereas there wasn't even one clergyman in the army of America's major ally, the atheistic Soviet Union. To the end, Hitler himself paid his church taxes. One must be careful not to confuse the thousand-year battle in Germany between "Kaiser" and "Church" for the greater rôle in the Reich — a battle that also went on throughout Hitler's reign — with an attempt to curtail the Christian religion. Martin Luther, the great German reformer, had fought the same battle four centuries before, and thereby laid the groundwork for Christian Protestantism.

5. *There is nothing in* Mein Kampf *that Hitler wanted to annihilate the Jews!* Actions before and during the war certainly were stringent, but *millions* of "Holocaust survivors" in Israel, in the United States, in the Soviet Union and elsewhere prove the absence of any "extermination" orders. Had such orders existed, would a sick and fragile, an unable to work Anne Frank have survived Auschwitz? Instead, she was eventually transported back across the Reich to a camp (Bergen-Belsen) that *until January 1945 (!)* had been used to transfer Jews to Switzerland and freedom. And, what kept the Germans from "exterminating" the thousands of Jews, among them many children, who had long been at Auschwitz, and who fell into Russian hands when the camp was liberated? Did they run out of "gas" or ammo?

No serious treatise on Adolf Hitler can be written without exploring the question as to the meaning of his existence, and his impact on mankind's future. To find valid answers we must first ask the question: *Who was Hitler?* It is easy to believe all the stories told during and since the end of the war and assume that he was the personification of evil. Believing this, no further thought is necessary. But there is also the fact that literally millions of people (far more than is generally assumed) are now secret admirers of the late Führer. Even for many young Americans he is a personality of *their* era, and not just some dead relic of past history. Modern communications, especially television, in their quest for sensationalism have accomplished the impossible: they had kept Adolf Hitler and his ideas alive. And the results of this "propaganda success" will be seen in the not too distant future.

The Belgian ex-Rexist leader and former SS-General, Leon Degrelle, now living in exile in Spain, recently wrote a book titled *Hitler, Born at Versailles*. Nothing could be more apt to describe this phenomenon (and there is no better word for Hitler) in a historical sense. *Without the harsh, demeaning and inhumane conditions of the Treaty of Versailles there would have been no Hitler* as we experienced him. It is even doubtful that the unknown World War I corporal would ever have entered politics—or, if he had, he would probably not have stuck with it but would have gone back to his beloved art or architecture.

Many person believe that Adolf Hitler was the embodiment of the German people of his era in one person. He said what he felt, he thought and acted—with their wholehearted consent—in their name, and he dreamt their dreams. No doubt Hitler was a superb orator who knew exactly how to appeal to the masses (a skill absolutely necessary for rallying the people against the Communist menace), but he could not have been as successful if his message had not been sincere. It bears remembering that Hitler could mingle freely and without fear among his well-armed soldiers as late as March 1945, when he visited the Oder front with barely a handful of officers.

What will be Hitler's impact on mankind's future? Barely half a century after his demise, the world order that was created after the destruction of the Third Reich is crumbling by itself. Most ideological edifices upon which this world had rested have proven unworkable and clearly outdated. International socialism (Marxism) is in its death throes, and will soon have fewer disciples in Russia than among American university professors. Current developments in

China, in the Soviet Union, and such countries as Yugoslavia point to a "national" socialism, albeit without the swastika. Internationalism, as a political institution, is still in power, as was proven by the most recent American election. The trend, however, is toward nationalism, another one of Hitler's basic principles. Looking at today's world in disarray, and reading of "ethnic" troubles in Armenia, Estonia, Latvia, Lithuania, Afghanistan and elsewhere, who can doubt that nationalism is gaining and internationalism is losing? Even the trade wars, just now in the beginning stage, prove this point. And vaunted democracy? Where does it really exist but in Switzerland? Dare we still call the American system, where the people have less chance to unelect "their" Congressional representatives than the Germans had to get rid of unwanted NSDAP "Reichstag" members, and where most of the media only permit certain "approved" ideas to be discussed, a democracy? The last major canon of Hitler's ideas pertains to race. Just reading American newspapers of the present we can see that race is again very much a matter of discussion, and that, especially among young American whites, racial consciousness is growing by leaps and bounds as a backlash to insatiable demands by "ethnic" minorities. If we are honest with ourselves, can we not see already where this will lead? Certainly, the "multi-cultural," "multi-ethnic" and "pluralistic" society contemplated by Hitler's adversaries has come to an end before it ever really started.

It becomes ever more clear that Hitler was a man of the future, and not the reactionary of the past, as he has been depicted so frequently. It is true that National Socialism, the ideology of the "Nazis," had not ripened by the time the war ended. The unanticipated, short development of the SS from a small "super-German" élite unit of a few thousand men to a million-man *European* Waffen-SS with a vastly different political and social outlook proves that best. It is ironic that Hitler never intended his ideas/ideology for export. He had even been hesitant to see National Socialism extend beyond German borders to Germany's closest neighbors (except in countries such as Holland, where the population is genetically German). Now a *world-wide* revival is taking place that even crosses racial lines.

As we enter the 1990s, and Hitler's second century, there is little doubt that the very pillars upon which his ideology rested, namely race, nationalism, National Socialism and the "Führerprinzip" (leadership principle), seem ideas of the future—not only in Europe but, especially, among the *peoples* of his major adversaries, the United States and the Soviet Union. Also, sciences such as genetics, eugenics, and environmentalism, that for decades had been unpopular because they had been an integral part of the National Socialist "Weltanschauung," are currently in vogue again. And, the most devastating result of the lost war, the unnatural division of Germany, seems, in historical perspective, about to come to an end—both of the superpowers are in economic, political, and military decline, and, most importantly, the German VOLK are, at last, beginning to stir from their slumber.

Where he alive today, Adolf Hitler would be pleased.

WIR SIND NICHT
DIE LETZTEN VON GESTERN
SONDERN
DIE ERSTEN
VON MORGEN

H SÜNDERMANN

20 April 1889　　　　*20 April 1989 — 28*　　　　*30 April 1945*

THE REAL MEANING OF HITLER GERMANY

Many of the things which happened in Europe in the 1920's and 1930's were simply beyond the ken of the average American. They reprented nothing which could be expressed in terms of the American experience. Even after the Great Depression struck in 1929, Americans were basically optimistic; they believed that with a little tinkering and horse sense, the world could be made to run successfully. Liberalism was still alive in America; it was utterly dead in Europe. Americans tended to label European happenings with familiar American labels. Thus when Hitler came along he was tagged a "Right Wing" political leader. Actually, Hitler was born into a world in which the terms "Left" and "Right" had ceased to have any real meaning. Europe had toiled under Rothschild oppression for a hundred years. Rothschild, the great Capitalist, was also the prime financial backer of Marxism. The corruption of Europe was complete. The Press, owned by Rothschild, thundered against the "Godless Proletariat." At the same time, lapdog intellectuals employed by Rothschild lured the European workers into Marxist movements, which were really "Company Unions" much addicted to making sweetheart contracts with Rotschild-backed interests. Europe was in the grip of a brilliant Jewish fraud.

Jewish writers almost always speak of "Hitlerism" as if it were the sole invention of a man named Adolf Hitler. Actually, when the masses go berserk there is always a little man who will get in front of them and run, and he is likely to be called their "Leader." The real essence of the matter is that the German masses had gone berserk under the lash of Rothschild oppression. It was possible to lead them, to guide them, but not to thwart their basic purpose. Why did the German masses demand the hide of the Jew? For the same reason that the masses everywhere demand the hide of the Jew: The Jew fancies himself a "World Aristocrat," destined to be leader and ruler of the world's masses. What will it take to convice the Jews that the world's masses do not want them and will not have them? The German experience ought to have made a profound change in the attitude of the Jews. If the Jews had the capability of learning from experience, they would now abdicate their positions of power in great Gentile nations; but the hubris of the modern Jew is apparently nearly indestructible.

The collision between the irresistible Jews and the immovable masses is the most spectacular head-on collision the world has ever seen. The Jew-Marxist intellectual prattles about "The Masses" but the Masses are the real enemies of the Jews. Marxism is not an effective lever by which the Jews can control the masses. Marxism was never stronger in any nation than in Germany. The strength of German Marxism had to be seen to be believed. You had to see the people of the working class districts of RED BERLIN going to the polls to elect a solidly Communist delegation to the Reichstag. The German workers were the Called and Chosen and Faithful of Marxism, the Vanguard of the Proletariat, the most advanced industrial working class in the world.

The German Jews counted upon Marxism to enable them to maintain their hold upon the country. At one time, the power of the German Jews was as great as the power of the New York Jews in America today. They almost owned Germany, and wealthy Jews poured out millions of marks to support Communism. Marxism in Germany then, as in America today, was a prime tool of Jewish power. It was used to manipulate not only the people of the Left

Kampfjahr 1929!

Wing, but also the people of the Right Wing. Life seemed to be a great debate over whether society should be organized along "Capitalist" or "Communist" lines; actually, there was no real conflict between Capitalism and Communism; the Jew-Capitalist and the Jew-Communist were blood brothers, mutually interested in a primordial racial battle against the *Goyim*, and not in the largely fictitious "Class Struggle."

Against this background, Gustav Krupp made an important decision. We happen to admire Krupp; but this is not the reason why we keep mentioning him. The fact is that he made a decision which will have to be made, one way or another, by dozens or hundreds of *Goyim* around the world: *Shall I throw in my lot with the Jews, or shall I throw in my lot with the masses of Gentiles?*" Krupp decided to throw in his lot with the German people, with the Gentile nation, rather than with the Jews. That is why Krupp backed Hitler. Every important Gentile leader in the world will have to make this decision sooner or later. The tendency in America is to straddle the fence; but this is a fence which cannot be straddled successfully.

Russian political leaders also have to make this decision: *"Shall we thrown in our lot with the Jews, or with the dark, primitive masses?"* This decision *has* to be made; it cannot be evaded. The stakes in the game are very high. The Jew promises that he can control *dark masses* with his bag of intellectual tricks; he can, so he says, control the vicious lusts, the burning passions of the animal-like herd. But what if the Jew can't do it? What if the *dark masses* simply run berserk and trample the Jews and their allies underfoot like a herd of stampeding cattle? The Jew says that the way to control the Masses is with his bag of intellectual tricks, which he invented in his spare time, when he was not busy peddling, pawnbroking or pants-pressing. The intelligent pragmatist is suspicious of the Jew; he knows in his heart that the real way to lead the masses it to get in front of them and run. The intellectual Jew propounds a very dubious position. It is against all of the experience of six thousand years of recorded history.

By 1925 the Jews had failed in Europe. To be young in Europe in those days was to know things which, to this day, are not well understood in America. There were young men in the cafés, whom you read about in *Harper's* or *Atlantic Monthly* or the *Saturday Review of Literature*. There were Hemingways and all of the glorious American expatriates of the romantic "Lost Generation." There were other young men whom you did not read about in

America. There were young men who talked of strange things, such "Rebarbarization." What would such a word have meant to Americans of the period? Nothing, I am sure. In Europe it meant the Wave of the Future. In America the Liberal Age was still alive; in Europe, it was quite dead. You saw it only as a shambles of ruins, beyond repair, beyond hope. In America it was possible to believe that Liberalism could be "saved." In Europe it was impossible to believe with any real conviction that it was worth saving. This was perfectly demonstrated when Hitler came along. The Jewish publishing executives pushed the important-looking buttons on their desks; prostitute writers came running to do their bidding. Phoney political cartoonists set out to fry and sizzle a little man named Adolf. The Jews had the power, or so they thought, to destroy a little upstart like Hitler, even if he was financed by Krupp and trained by Von Papen. The Jewish campaign against Hitler never got off the ground in Europe. The fingers of the cartoonists became palsied over their drawing boards. The writers, always before so glib and willing in their literary prostitution to the Jews, found themselves unable to write anything effective against Hitler. There were always those thousands of voices outside the window crying "HEIL HITLER! SIEG HEIL!" The Jewish will wilted and collapsed. The Jews still do not understand the reality of men like Hitler and Mussolini. The real importance of Adolf Hitler is not to be found within the individual person named Adolf; Adolf Hitler is important because there are eighty million of him. He represents the masses clamoring for liberation from Jewish rule. He represents the *power of the majority*. The Jew stands for snide intellectual trickery and shoddy minority politics; Hitler is the man who gets in front of the majority and runs. The Jew can manipulate ambitious and mediocre little men, who want public office and public honor bought with Jewish money; the Jew cannot manipulate the majority.

There are, on the public scene today, a great many funny little men who think that they can manipulate the masses by means of mass propaganda. The Masses are a great, blind, stampeding herd; they will trample indifferently all of the funny little men who try to

Horst Weffel in Nürnberg 1929

Am 9. Oktober
Horst Weffel 30 Jahre alt

Archiv: Hoffmann

Deutsch sein heißt:

Treu sein –
Wahr sein –
Kämpfer sein.

Und Kämpfer sollt ihr sein,
Kämpfer für alles Gute und Schöne.

Dazu Heil!   Horst Wessel

manipulate them. Being "for" or "against" the power of the masses is futility; it is like being "for" or "against" tidal waves, earthquakes, or volcanoes. In any case, what are you going to do about such matters? What do you do when it rains? You just let it rain. What will you do when the Masses stampede and trample the Jews? You will do well to keep out of their way.

We are not guessing about this. We saw it happen in Europe in the 1920's and the 1930's. Hitler's final defeat by forces from outside Europe has obscured the totality of his victory within Europe. Hitler did not conquer Europe; Europe threw itself into Hitler's hands. Jewish writers often romanticize about the "underground opposition" to Hitler in Europe during World War II. The fact about the "opposition" to Hitler is that there was none. The rotten old House of Cards built by Rothschild had collapsed. There was no intellectual fortress of Liberalism which even tried to stand against Hitler. Marxism? Anybody who missed the collapse of Marxism in "Red Berlin" missed one of the great spectacles of history. One day in the 1930's I strolled through the Brandenburg Tor, and along Unter den Linden, and saw a parade. I saw a band of husky young men marching in brown shirts with Swastika armbands.

I knew most of them personally. I had seen them before at Communist meetings. They were the Called and Chosen and Faithful of Marxism, the Vanguard of the Proletariat; and here they were, marching with Swastika armbands. "Red Berlin" joined the Nazi Party, practically to the last man. I have never had any faith in the staying-power of Marxism since. Often I hear Communist or anti-Communist gasbags speaking as if the world really *must choose* between Capitalism and Communism. I saw the young men of Berlin make their choice; they did not choose Capitalism or Communism; they chose brown shirts with Swastika armbands. They quickly forgot how to sing *The International* or *The Red Flag* and learned to sing a new song called *The Horst Wessel Lied*. The Age of Rotschild was over. It was foolish even to use such words as "Left" or "Right" in connection with such a matter; all such political words really belonged to a past age. Now we can see clearly the limitation of the modern Jew. He can manipulate world affairs successfully only as long as the direction of world affairs remains in the hands of a creative minority; thus the circumstances which built Jewish power in the Nineteenth Century were almost entirely accidental. The Jew was a mere parasite in a system not of his own creation. He cannot stand alone; and, as he has destroyed his competitors of the Gentile Élite, he is left more and more to stand alone. When he stands alone at his pinnacle of power, his incompetence is brutally revealed. He cannot cope with the masses. Marxism was supposed to be an ideology for the masses, but it has remained largely the hobby of the professional intellectuals. Adolf Hitler disposed of German Marxism almost effortlessly. He did not do this because he possessed occult powers, but because Marxism was about finished in any case, and the masses were already demanding somebody to lead them out of it. Hitler was a true leader; he got in front of the Masses and ran. He made the decision which every world leader must make: Shall I resist the masses or shall I give in to them?

It is the Jew today who seeks to dominate the world's masses, to boss them, to tyrannize over them, to defeat and channelize their desires. This is why the masses hate the Jew. Their hatred is bone-deep, violent, irrational, unthinking, instinctive. The Jew cannot argue with them because he cannot really communicate with them at all. The modern Jew is a great fool for standing in their way. When he stands in their way the masses will trample him and never even notice him.

Can such a thing really happen?

It did happen in Europe in the 1920's and the 1930's. It seems to us likely to happen around the world in the 1970's and the 1980's. *Common Sense* would prefer to see Jewish power replaced by orderly and capable Gentile leadership in large Gentile nations like the U.S.A. This does not, however, seem to be happening. The Gentile masses, abandoned by the sold-out traitors of their own race, who have become Judaized and have abandoned their responsibilities, are now like a herd of bison stampeding. They will solve "The Jewish Problem" with great finality, but the process is not likely to be an orderly, happy, or constructive one. This is because the old-line Gentile leadership have failed to lead their people, have failed to resist the Jews. The masses will find new leaders, and they may not insist that such leaders shall be entirely laudable; they will only insist upon being led against the Jews. In the near-term future, the world most likely faces a time of irrational violence, which will continue at the demand and insistence of the masses until Jewish power is liquidated.

If you want a preview of what will happen, simply look at Germany during the 1920's and 1930's. Germany was the test laboratory of tomorrow. You would think that the Jews would have learned something from Germany; since they have not, the world will gather its forces and make another effort to educate them. The leadership classes of the Gentiles have failed to resist the Jewish take-over of the world; now it will be the turn of the savage masses. The masses in the raw are seldom mild. If you want to be their leader in the coming times, you will have to get in front of them and run. If you want to try to resist them or control them, you will soon find that you are always running around with Jews. Can the funny little Jew really divert the stampeding masses?

Tune in on the years from the 1970's to the 1980's for the breath-taking answer. This drama promises to be exciting, to say the least.

Common Sense, 1 February 1969

AMERICANA

Swastikas symbolized Good Luck in 1908 presidential election between
William Howard Taft and William Jennings Bryan.

20 April 1889   **20 April 1989 — 37**   *30 April 1945*

Die Alte Garde

Ich halte Umschau bei der Alten Garde,
Die einst mit mir deutsch treu gekämpft, geschafft
Wo sind sie hin, die Hüter der Standarte?
Die meisten hat der Tod hinweggerafft.
Sie, die mit mir im Männerkreise saßen
Bei ernstem deutschen Wort und deutschem Wein,
Die Alten Helden deckt der grüne Rasen
Und ich bin einsam — einsam und allein.

Mir fehlt die Kraft zu alter Warte stufen,
Dem Arm entsank die sieggewohnte Wehr
Doch will die Jungen ich zur Fahne rufen:
Wir brauchen Männer! Darum Männer her!
Wo sind die Sprossen alter Deutscher Eichen,
Die sich an diesem hehren deutschen Tag
Im Geist der Väter treu die Hände reichen
Und schwören, daß die Welt es hören mag:

,,Wir wollen deutsch sein, wie's die Alten waren,
Treu deutscher Sprache, deutscher Sitte traut!
Wir wollen fest stehen trotz der Welt Gefahren
Und schützen was der deutsche Geist erbaut.
Was uns die alte Heimat mitgegeben,
Sei treu gepflegt im neuen Vaterland.
Wir tragen's dieser neuen Welt in's Leben,
Hier, wo der Deutsche — kämpfend — Heimat fand.''

Schlaft wohl, Ihr Alten! Ihr habt ausgerungen;
Ihr schaut nicht mehr den Irrsinn dieser Welt,
Ihr hört nicht mehr die schmutz'gen Lästerzungen,
Ihr seht den Giftpfeil nicht auf uns geschnellt.
Des Deutschenhasses Wogen uns umbranden,
Der Lüge Schlangenbrut, die uns bedroht,
Und ringsumher in allen, allen Landen,
Dem Deutschen kündet Untergang und Tod.

Steht auf, Ihr Jungen, füllt der Alten Lücken!
Noch ist es Zeit, setzt mutig euch zur Wehr!
Errichtet Dämme, bauet neue Brücken,
Stahlfest und dauernd, wie der Schutz am Meer.
Ihr Jungen Sprossen deutscher Eichenriesen,
Seid auf das Werk der Alten Garde stolz —
Die nie im Schoß die Hände ruhen ließen,
Sie schnitzten euch aus deutschem Eichenholz.

The above poem was published on 25 June 1939 in the Chicago *Sonntagspost* on the occasion of *German Day* 1939. Name of author unknown

Bei den Sternen steht,
was wir schwören;
der die Sterne lenkt,
wird uns hören:
eh der Fremde dir
deine Kronen raubt,
Deutschland, fallen wir
Haupt bei Haupt.

Heilig Vaterland,
heb zur Stunde
kühn dein Angesicht
in die Runde.
Sieh uns all entbrannt,
Sohn bei Söhnen stehn:
Du sollst bleiben, Land!
Wir vergehen!

Heilig Vaterland,
in Gefahren
deine Söhne stehn
dich zu wahren.
Von Gefahr umringt,
heilig Vaterland,
schau, von Waffen blinkt
jede Hand.

R. A. Schröder

UNDER THE SWASTIKA

GERMANY SERVES NOTICE

Viscount Rothermere, brother of Lord Northcliffe, and owner of the *Daily Mail* in England, the fearless British newspaper magnate, well known for his stand, favoring the revision of the

---

20 April 1889   **20 April 1989 − 40**   *30 April 1945*

treaty of Versailles, and the return of the colonies to Germany, has taken a definite stand in support of the Nazi Government in Germany. He advises the young and progressive Britishers to pay most careful attention to New Germany, and to disregard misleading and adverse reports. He significantly remarks, that it would be of tremendous benefit to Britain, if Hitler could be thought of as being an Englishman.

Similarly, Lord Noel Buxton, in a letter to the *London Times,* refers to Hitler as one of the greatest men of the century.

One must look behind the scenes, penetrate into the heart and mind of the average young German of today, to comprehend what is taking place, and what is behind this glowing modern German self-assertion, what is at the root of anti-Semitism, and what determined Germany to sidestep the alien elements. And, even then, no clear idea can be had, unless we understand, also, the political and social atmosphere of pre-war Germany, and feel the hidden resentments, which grew out of the pyramiding of grievances, disenfranchisements, favoritisms to alien elements, special privileges, by an irresponsible government, which finally led to revolution, and the fall of the Dynasty.

It is unfortunate for the Americans that the Jewish problem has introduced into an otherwise exceedingly profitable discussion a confusing and quarrelsome element, so that the main issues, to which the Jewish question is but of minor importance, have become befogged. However, since the Jewish question has assumed national and international proportions, it is necessary to deal with it, and to dispose of it, so that the road be cleared for an intelligent, unbiased approach to the Hitler political-economy.

Antagonism against the Jews has existed in Germany for many years, but never developed into anything worse than a battle of words. Right along, the Jews had it all their own way, economically, financially, politically. It was not until Bolshevism began to grow in Germany, that it was found that the true face of Bolshevism was a Jewish one. It was Bolshevism that forced the Jews in Germany into the open. For the measures enacted against the Bolshevists, predominantly, though unintentionally, hit the Jews. It was this Bol-shevistic affiliation that turned out to be very unfortunate for Judah; because, in the eyes of the world it justifies the sternest measures Germany might take to rid herself of the Jewish-Bolshevist menace. In a similar manner, this war, fought by Judah with a special kind of poison-gas, which by way of newspapers is spreading like a pestilen-tial miasma into every nook and cranny of the land, will finally prove to be a boomerang in this double-barreled boycott of goods and blood. The fate of the Jews in Germany requires most careful consideration, they are in a very exposed position. Wisdom, if not charity, demands that the Jews temper their passions with a goodly portion of Jewish sagacity, lest a more acute situation be created. It is well to let sleeping dogs lie.

So far as Germany's relations to the Jews is concerned, she resents, and will obstruct to the utmost, the notorious, aggressive, ruthless, anti-social Jewish tactics and business activities, rather than object to the presence of a few thousand individual Jews in Germany. She is determined to break the strangle-hold of predatory Jewish groups upon Germany. this makes racial qualifications necessary. If personal offense be taken, it can come only from those who are not in a position to grasp the bearing of the Jewish problem upon German national life. This problem cannot be permitted to degenerate into a conflict of personalities, and so far as Germany is concerned, it is a conflict of antagonistic racial tradi-tions, customs, habits. Germany's position needs no defense. Her internal affairs are inviolably her own; to interfere would be an affront. And, lest it be overlooked, Germany finally decided upon "What is to be," only after those whose interests were involved had ample opportunity of determining, to a degree, "What might have been." Now the time of compromise has passed; and the wisest course, for those adversely affected, is to avoid the arising of fur-ther restrictions. The Jews in Germany, who are feeling the heavy hand, must thank themselves for that result, having failed to curb the anti-social and anti-national activities of the predatory groups within their own race. In connection with this, it is difficult to understand why Jewry still should make the fight of the Jewish-Russian and Polish Communists her own, and consequently, invite additional reprisals and restrictive legislation against the domiciled Jews of Germany. Unless it be in the forlorn hope of forcing the German leaders into a compromise. This is badly mistaking the temper of the Nazis. New Germany is exceedingly conscious of being honour-bound to carry through. There is an ominous, emotional intensity in this resolution which, though born of desperation, nevertheless has been carefully tempered by keen and sober insight.

The Hitler movement demands the closest attention, for its effects will be felt the world over; every government will have to reckon with it, make no mistake about that. There is something uncompromising about this movement. It scrapes the bed-rock of economic and political thought and, whether we embrace or reject, we must keep its innate driving power in mind.

Personal profits? Individual aggrandisement? There is none of this for anyone in particular, but the world at large will profit enormously. For the Hitler movement is bent upon reconciling national and economic differences. This may sound paradoxical to Jewish ears. Nevertheless, from the reconciliation of national differences, the economically small Jew stands to gain as much as the economically small German. Under the Versailles Treaty, the small Jew in Germany, sooner or later, would have starved like other thousands of small Germans. The Jews who ultimately will find themselves in Palestine, likely will thank their stars for having escaped a holocaust. For wars are still in the air, Hitlerism is not yet old enough to prevent them. Nations are not yet done with sending their industrious and productive citizens, ignorant of any insult, and innocent of any wrong done, away from plough and bench, to kill, or to be killed, by similarly industrious and productive, ignorant and innocent, citizens of another nation, for God knows what. Wars leave scars, and there are none worse than the resentments bred by wars.

Hitler wants to reconcile these resentments, wants to show that racial and national resentments always have been inoculated by deception for purposes of profit, or aggrandisement. The decent citizen of any one country harbors no hate for the decent citizens of another country, unless he has been misled, into disbelieving his own heart and natural instincts.

The innocent inhabitants of every country always have had to struggle against being victimized by dishonest politicians, and by those in control of wealth and power. Wars provide opportunities for plunder; plunder, with methodical thoroughness, is going on everywhere, and little difference is made, whether the victims be Jew or Gentile.

Socialism and radicalism are attempts to get away from these impositions by power and wealth. Yet, in his eagerness for reform the radicalist is often tempted to throw out the baby with the bathwater. Nationalism, in its prostituted form, is chauvinism. The radicals ignore the virtues of true national sentiments that are buried under an overburden of viciousness. Internationalism is no sentiment, is unnatural, cannot be felt, is a mere intellectual concept. National and racial differences are never resented by any man, they are cultivated because they are interesting. No matter how humble the hovel in which we spent our childhood, we love it more than a pretentious palace. National sentiment is only a broader home-sentiment. Why destroy something that harbors no element of contention?

Nationalism grows into a bugaboo only when hidden political cliques, within the legitimate national government, destroy the peace of the nation, and arouse an open, or concealed, resentment against treachery. A nation is diseased in which an insignificant minority ravishes, and economically, financially, and politically engulfs the population. Whether this dispossession be practiced, legally by so-called constitutional rulers, or underhandedly by a group of bankers or industrialists, is in the end a matter of indifference. Socialism can be in harmony with national spirit and sharp individual and racial distinctions. Individualism and ownership of property are fountain-heads of energy and initiative, they give a nation its very life,they do not constitute a danger, so long as private ownership, and personal initiative, are prohibited from growing into instruments of power for plundering the weaker elements of society, not merely of what they legitimately acquired in material wealth, but also of the opportunities for preserving, and acquiring, a cultural heritage.

Modern society, even now, prohibits possessing oneself of property by means of theft, fraud, or murder, but it still legally permits taking away the property of another by a cunningly constructed banking- or stock-exchange technique; a legal form of fraud and theft. It cannot be denied that constantly conditions are arising which are beyond the control of the debtor, such as business depressions, overproduction, unstable seasons, disease, death; nevertheless, the law of the land places all of these risks upon the shoulders of the debtor, and permits the creditor, regardless of these conditions, to sell out his debtor by giving him the power of "expropriating the owner." This form of legalized theft and fraud will find no support in new Germany; personal interests shall not jeopardize common interests.

In the New Germany the interests in the soil, by the honest tiller of the soil, shall be encouraged by guaranteeing him perpetual ownership of that soil, and by protecting him against unjust abuses, now practiced far and wide by "interest-sharks." Rapacity, usury, spoliation, and dishonest political practices are rampant in every country on earth. In Germany they shall become a dangerous profession; the laborer shall be guaranteed his profits; the criminal his deserts. Confidence in a responsible government again shall become established among the people, honest labor not be abused, profiteering and craftiness not bring a premium; ideal values find an opportunity of better appreciation and compensation, and the tendency of everything becoming the property of one man, of a small group of men, shall be broken.

The German insistence upon racial qualifications has an unexpectedly important aspect, aside from that of racial purity. Since alien elements are prevented from entering the German national structure, notice is given to the world that Germany has no interest in conquering or subjugating others for the purpose of incorporating them into her own national body. This policy will tend to establish neighborly and international confidence.

The New Germany intends to concentrate upon a peaceful, intensive, internal development, and looks forward to equally peaceful, commercial activities abroad, and not to an inconsiderate drive for markets by methods of underselling, or an undesirable concentration upon cheap goods, both of which endanger the security and happiness of the productive and industrial classes of other nations, and in the end must lead to enmities and jealousies among nations, as well as to a deterioration of German standards.

Germany having been stripped to the bone, materially, instinctively reacts by accentuating her traditions and ideals. Inexorably, she is driven to step beyond material values, to create an intensified German ideal. "Germany Over All," today has assumed a deeper meaning. The interests of her nationals, the very existence of the German race, demand a fiery, even fanatic, cultivation of the German ideals, no matter what material values be at stake. To sin in this direction is national suicide.

THE GERMAN NATIONAL-SOCIALIST PROGRAM

This party program constitutes an extraordinary political document, insofar as it is reinforced by the pledge of the party leaders to carry this twenty-five-point party program to its realization, regardless of whatever dangers to the life of the leaders may be incurred in the process.

1. Union of all Germans, wherever located, on the basis of the self-determination of all nations.
2. Cancellation of the Treaty of Versailles and St. Germain.
3. Return of colonies.
4. German racial qualification to be a condition of German citizenship.

5. Nationals not of German blood cannot be German citizens, they may live in Germany as visitors, subject to special rules.

6. German officials must be of German blood.

7. The German State is obligated to provide opportunities for the support of all of its citizens.

8. Deportation of all aliens that entered Germany since August 2, 1914.

9. Equal rights and equal obligations for all.

10. Common welfare to precede personal welfare, under all conditions.

11. Removal of abuses incident to the institution of capital and interest.

12. Confiscation of all War profits.

13. State ownership of existing trusts.

14. State participation in the major business concerns.

15. Old-age pension for every citizen.

16. Encouragement of private initiative, suppression of department stores.

17. Reform of land laws, with preference to private ownership, expropriation without compensation of lands that have been neglected or are being held for speculation, or have been fraudulently acquired.

18. Relentless suppression of the criminal element, death penalty for usurers, profiteers, corrupt officials.

19. German laws to replace existing Roman laws in Germany.

20. Opportunity for every talented German child to acquire an education which will fit him to fill the highest office in the state; especial emphasis to be placed upon civic and political training.

21. Protection of home, mother and child, removal of women from the industrial field, prohibition of child labor, universal athletic training.

22. Citizen guard in place of conscription.

23. Libel laws, especially to curb political abuses. A German

press, requiring purely German staff; non-Germans cannot financially support a German press. Non-Germans are prohibited from printing newspapers or books in the German language, unless marked "Translations," and by special permit.

24. Religious liberty, so long as the teaching does not collide with the moral sentiments of the German race.

25. Unqualified authority of the central office of the Reich over Germany's policies and each and every German organization. Abolition of parliamentary government, in place of which a leader system, based upon the principle of "Authority to those below, Responsibility to those above."

The leader, Adolf Hitler, has been given a a four-years General Power of Attorney for the purpose of putting this program into effect. At the end of these four years a new vote by the people will decide whether these policies shall be continued by the same leader, or whether other policies and other leaders shall guide the destiny of the Reich thereafter.

THE ROOTS OF THE
GERMAN-JEWISH CONFLICT

No problem can be solved until its roots are fully exposed to view. The roots of the German-Jewish conflict lie in the fact that the Jews do not maintain a national domicile, preferring to live among host-nations instead. Now, all races are so constituted that they consider every stranger as racially inferior, and that sentiment is based upon the very sound instincts that all men are *not* born equal, that racial differences cannot be ignored. Although the United States of America bases her constitution upon the assumption that all men are born equal, she, nevertheless, rigidly excludes from her shores three quarters of the population of the earth. The Jews are admitted, they belong. Therefor, a Jewish problem, as it arose under Hitler in Germany, cannot be constitutionally justified in the United States of America. Here, race is second to nationality, while in Germany race and nation are one. Hence, what is true of the United States cannot be true of Germany, a fact well worth remembering.

Powerful racial structures have been completely wrecked, and their civilization destroyed, by thoughtless admission of alien elements; the empires of Greece and Rome, drastically and tragically, bear mute witness to this fact. Foreign elements in large numbers, during the past, have been introduced into the German stock, but they have been absorbed, or shed, and no longer present a racial problem. The Jews have remained a detached racial fraction of the German population for over 1600 years. That is time enough to conclusively demonstrate that the German is incapable of assimilating the Jew. There is nothing at all offensive in this; diverging racial qualities are characteristics; they are neither virtues, nor vices. White does not make a rose more beautiful than red. The mixing of otherwise agreeable odors may produce a very disagreeable hotchpotch. In Germany, the door to economic equality, and available cultural facilities, was always open to the Jews. In fact, the Jews established an economic superiority in Germany. From that to political control was but a step. Yet, it cannot be taken without coming into serious conflict with the traditions of the host-nation. But the Jews took that step, regardless. They made a dive for possessing themselves of the national structure of the host. They believed their economic control of Germany would be a match to the strength of the German racial spirit. They were mistaken.

Germany never imposed racial inferiority upon the Jews. Racial equality cannot be bestowed; it is a matter of birth and inheritance, not one of immigration. One cannot possess, one cannot make use of, racial characteristics unless one racially belongs.

Furthermore, leaving racial considerations entirely aside, if a fraction of a population studiously, or involuntarily, remains a separate racial unit within a nation, it thereby forfeits every national claim on that nation. To become nationally attached or related to a country, such as the United States of America, the consciousness of racial superiority must be subjected to the consciousness of national superiority. But in Germany, there can be neither racial nor national attachment for any foreigner; there can be only a national association, a relationship of host and guest. The inherent weakness of the Austrian Empire lay in the fact that various alien groups, constituting the nation, could not subject their racial consciousness to a common, pronounced Austrian national consciousness. For the Jew to demand racial equality from the Germans would be an equality shot through and through with self-deception. The German among the Germans, as the Jew among the Jews, always remains racially superior to any foreigner. One cannot buy, sell, borrow something that must be inherited. It would be painting a white lily red; the famous sale of the first birthright for a pottage of lentils to the contrary not withstanding. The Jewish problem will disappear as soon as the Jews learn to idealize their own national country, as the German does his.

THE CLASH OF GERMAN AND JEWISH TRADITIONS

There are villains among Jews and Gentiles who create misery and annoyance for their own people because of unsocial activities. The Jews like to identify themselves with unpatriotic and internationally-minded organizations; as a consequence, the better class Jew is kept in hot water and forced into a position of defense.

Though this thing has been going on as far back as we can think, the better class Jew does not go out of his way to curb these vicious tendencies of his co-nationals.

It was not until some wealthy Jews were caught smuggling out of Germany and across the borders of Switzerland and Holland valises brimful with bills of exchange that atrocity stories began to be broadcast.

To smuggle gold across the border would constitute a similar offense in America. Such gold would be subject to confiscation by the United States Government, and the offender would be punished besides.

By this time you have been fed-up with "manufactured to order" atrocity stories, as you are already with the "cut-off-hands" stories from Belgium.

While the cables were kept hot with descriptions of terrible outrages, you looked upon them as just another Jewish pogrom to be added to the long list of others that from time immemorial have been wreaked upon the innocent Jews, wherever they pitched their tents, be it in Egypt, Persia, Babylon, Cyprus, Rome, Spain, England, France, Poland, and Germany.

The United States of America herself has deported 4,500 Communistic Jews, without raising any hubbub at home or abroad. Maybe the United States are too close to home, and the evidence too disserviceable to the Jewish cause in the United States, to make it advisable to spread this information over the country.

How unfortunate we lack the faculty of reading the other fellow's thought, his intrigues and schemes. But in her infinite wisdom, providence has decreed that the thoughts of Jews and Gentiles alike shall be read by deeds. Protestations of friendship and patriotism mean little, so long as deeds have not justified the faith.

Faith-tradition-breeding-character-blood are essentially one. If you want to know a person, a family, a race, study the traditional inheritance.

What do we mean by tradition?

The manners and customs of a family or a race, handed down from generation to generation, and acted upon so long as to become an unwritten law.

It represent the product of a careful process of nursing, it originated in hospitality, and, in the last analysis, in an expression of faith and confidence, a test of traditional qualities.

It is the foundation of virtue and racial pride, of racial consciousness itself; it is the soil in which comradeship, charity, chivalry grow. Where traditions clash there can be no harmony among people. That is the reason why Germans and Jews cannot agree.

Even among the lowest of races, to outrage hospitality is an unpardonable offense, and frequently punished by death; rightly so, because it invariably points to depravity of character, to utter lack of traditional qualities.

The Jews, who directed the political racket in Germany, employed the gangster-methods of the Russian-Jewish Bolsheviks, and this Jewish-Bolshevism is determined upon uprooting every national and traditional bond. Millions of Russians, who resisted this juggernaut of the Jewish-Bolshevistic regime, and fought for their traditional inheritance, were summarily executed.

A similar fate was to be provided for Germany, and during the pre-Hitler days Germany received a fair sample of it. Had Bolshevism been introduced into Germany then, there would have been no trumped up atrocities, but real ones. The Germanic stock would have been reduced by millions, and the Jews would have been that many ahead. The Germans were to get the same poisonous medicine previously spooned out to the Russians.

Ruthless trampling down of racial privileges and racial qualities of others is a typically Jewish policy, and because of it, the Jew is held in scorn.

It was part of the scheme of the Bolshevistic German-Jews to draw into Germany an army of Communistic Jews from Poland, Galizia, and Russia, and by supplying hundreds of thousands of these radical Jews with letters of German citizenship, the strongholds of the German-Jewish-radicalism in Berlin and other cities were to be reinforced. The official hoodlums expected that the control of the German government would fall into their lap like a ripe plum, and in certain expectation of this they made themselves broad in every governmental office, and supplanted German officials by Jewish Communists.

This brood, that lavished letters of citizenship by the hundreds of thousands upon a horde of alien Jews, denied a man like Hitler, a man of German blood, though of Austrian birth, the right to German citizenship, to which by virtue of blood he was inalienably

---

entitled. Hitler, who voluntarily had entered the German Army, had fought at the front and been wounded, had again returned to the front, and again been wounded, and for his bravery had received the Iron Cross of the First and Second Order, was denied his letter of citizenship!

Is there anything more pregnant of evil intent, more indicative of the callous disregard of national honor and tradition, anything that could better identify the character of those smirking Jew-Communists who sat with mocking leers in every office of Government, State, and Municipality of Germany?

Who can deny that the native Jews of Germany were not fully acquainted with what was going on, nor that they did not stir a finger to stay the hand of Judah-run-amuck?

Over half a million of Jews in Germany, and not enough appreciation of German traditions among the one-half million Jews to indignantly protest the outrages. The contemplation of this fact reveals an appalling moral and spiritual brutification.

What wonderful opportunity for the "German" Jew to give evidence to the world of the nobility of his Jewish nation, and the soundness of his Jewish traditions! How the Jew might have put even many a German to shame!

Such then is the receipt, the balancing of accounts, the Jews gave Germany in return for unparalleled advantages received from the German schools, universities, and cultural environments, not to mention business and lucre. Such was the return compliment a Jewish guest paid his host!

The question is in place: Why did the "supposedly decent" Jewish element in Germany permit the Jewish-gangster element to make a drive for the control of the German Government? Because the Jews in Germany fully expected this Jewish Communistic onslaught to be as successful there as it previously had been in Russia.

The Jews hate to go to Palestine! They dreamt of a new Palestine in Central Europe! Hitler spoiled that dream. That is reason enough to hate him!

How could such miscalculations happen to Judah? For the simple reason that 1,600 years sojourn among the Germans finds the Jew still as "un-German" as before, still with his insane greed for money, for power, for control, for monopoly, for tyranny.

German tradition? He is not interested. It is not in his blood.

ANTI-SEMITISM IS SYMPTOM, NOT CAUSE

Germany has among her population approximately 615,000 Jews; that is, one Jew to 100 Germans.

Accordingly, the Jewish element should be found in the various trades, occupations, professions, public offices, military institutions, universities, schools, in cities and country, and among the criminals and deserters, as 1 Jew to 100 Germans.

But, we find the Jews crowding together, gravitating to ghettos of their own making.

200,000 of them are in Berlin alone; the rest in cities, such as Frankfurt-Main, Hamburg, Bremen, Breslau, etc.

The Germans cannot assimilate the Jews, although Jews have been in German lands for over 1600 years.

The Jew is not fond of hard work, as the following figures show.

Farmers, including families	6,150
Industrials, do.	135,000
Commerce and traders, do.	338,250
Professionals, do.	36,900

The Jew wants to run things. It will be no surprise to find that at the time of the Jewish-German Chancellor, Rathenau, fully 80% of the most important Governmental offices in Germany were filled by Jews. We may assume that the resulting resentment among the Germans, probably, had some influence upon his assassination.

The officers of the First German Revolutionary Government is represented by a list of Jews; the Reichs-Conference of 1918, likewise received Jewish representatives from every State of the German Union.

Ambassador Luther said, at Mount Vernon, New York, May 24, 1933, "The reason for the anti-Jewish feeling in Germany is the fact that, while the Jews represent only 1% of the population, nearly 50% of the Governmental offices are occupied by Jews."

Bernard H. Ridder, owner of the New York *Staatszeitung*, returning from his trip to Germany on June 8, 1933, reported, "that 62% of all German Governmental offices are occupied by Jews."

Even under Emperor Wilhelm, in 1914, that is before the War, there were among 100 University professors 30 Jews. If we consider that the University professors are appointed, it throws a glaring light upon the Emperor's, and his advisors', unawareness of the Jewish menace in Germany; or it exposes him to the criticism of "un-German" policies, and inferentially, to the accusation of unfairness to his people.

The Jewish influence in German affairs steadily continued to grow, so that in 1932 there were among 100 professors in medicine 45 Jews, in law 47. This condition practically amounted to a monopoly of the professions, and notably of the legal, since it introduced a strange and disquieting Jewish influence into the German judiciary.

Incidentally, worse conditions existed in Vienna. There were to every 100 in the professions, of physicians 80 Jews, of attorneys 84, of dentists 89.

The cause of this intolerable and depressing abandonment of every one of the professions to the Jews is to be found in the following:

The haughty and clannish German ruling and professional class connived in a systematic repression of any tendency of the financially less-fortunate Germans to go in for professional vocations. The German popular mind coined a saying, more in sarcasm than in joke, "there are no humans below an officer." One of the most vicious institutions was the one-year-military-service-privilege for those of a certain degree of education, while upon the ordinary soldier, who could not afford that privilege, a two or three years military term was imposed.

These policies of chicanery towards the middle and lower classes, successfully reserved for the clans a certain prestige, because of these hereditary privileges.

To the average German, regardless of his character or intellectual qualifications, the door to advancement, to higher education, to a military or a governmental career was successfully and ruthlessly shut.

True to tradition, the average German had confidence in the judgement of his leaders, he did not question their wisdom, never suspected clannish motives; he interpreted as "necessary policies" what at bottom was barefaced "selfishness and hypocrisy."

Those who knew better became dissatisfied with the existing injustice, but for evident reasons were helpless; they had to eat crow, or leave the country; and in fact many did leave.

Germany as a result suffered in two ways; she raised expensive and valuable human material, only to lose it to other countries, that reaped the benefit; besides, she alienated the affections of many of her own people.

The school system in Germany cunningly disregarded the interests of the middle and lower classes. It was constructed to prevent them from following a professional career; those who nursed such aspirations were frightened away by the bugaboo of a threatening professional over-supply.

The German was subject to certain traditional inhibitions, not so the Jew, who took his own counsel, or likely, took his people's advice. And, how could the Jews in Germany overlook a condition admirably suited to their needs; a condition that did not require hatching, but was ready-made for them. They saw an opportunity to supply that from which the German competitor was being deliberately driven away, and kept away, by those who directed the policies of Germany's educational methods, and who were, traditionally, notoriously numb to the needs of the common people, and their most vital interests.

Of course, under Wilhelm, "Lehrfreiheit" and "Lernfreiheit," the freedom to teach and to learn, was widely stimulated among the select, the rest of the people had to content themselves with "Lehrzwang" and "Lernzwang," a stereotyped educational discipline, in which "Lehrfreude" and "Lernfreude," the joy of teaching and learning, was all but killed.

In this manner, the average German was deliberately cheated out of his birthright, and by the very ones who expected from him "loyalty to death"; meanwhile, and without especial effort, the professional plumes fell into the hands of the Jews.

Although, these educational policies have been considerably changed in recent years, these facts must be told, however disagreeable their relation may be to a German. For without a clear understanding of the conditions as they existed previous to the war, and previous to the Revolution, and previous to Hitler, the present thoughts, sentiments, and reactions of the mass of the Germans cannot be understood, nor their attitude towards the Jews. The average German had come to feel like a stranger in his own land, and among his own people, where the weakness of the German leaders had become the strength of the Jews.

Anti-Semitism arose in German lands and principalities generations ago, when the German potentates, the descendants of the "robberknights" of yore, sold the rights of usury to the Jews and shared in the profits, which ran from 30 to 80% and more, and doubled upon defaulting. It was a common occurrence that a ridiculously small loan grew under the increasing interests to such an extent that often the entire property fell to the Jew, and the owner, together with his family, was sold into serfdom until loan and interest were paid.

But modern anti-Semitism has become acute since the War. Indeed, paradoxical though it sounds, anti-Semitism and Communism were at the root of the German Revolution, and hastened the termination of the war. It seems wherever the Jew is involved, we are dealing with paradoxes.

The Emperor was friendly to the Jews, he thought he had to depend upon Jews to adjust the existing conflict between his own, private Hohenzollern-family traditions and the public, German National traditions.

Likely, the thought never occurred to him that, as ruler of the Germans, the interests of the common people should be in the focus of his attention, and the glory of the private Hohenzollern traditions should be incidental, and secondary, to the glory of the German Public National traditions and the happiness of the people.

To him, the common people were mere "props to the throne" to whom it was a privilege to bleed and die on the battle field, so that the position of the Hohenzollerns be secure.

The Jew had the confidence of the Kaiser, and since the professional element in the German communities was thoroughly Jewish, the Jew claimed, as government-official, Kommerzienrat, physician or attorney, the confidence also of the people, and, as we shall see later, the expected happened, this confidence, both of the Kaiser and people, was finally betrayed.

The Jew is symptom, not cause; "Judaism is no religion, it is calamity," in the words of the Jewish poet Heinrich Heine.

Such is the picture, the result of a people's alienation; an alienation as outrageous as it was unnecessary and without parallel in history. It was a betrayal with a vengeance.

The Jew gained an increasing influence upon the political life of Germany, ever since the introduction of the parliamentary system in 1948, a consequence of the German revolution, the results of which mainly benefited the radical parties. The decade following is well remembered for the merciless persecution of Germany's finest, national-minded men. Hundreds of them were driven out of the country, and many more served long terms in prison. The dream of these men of German Unity temporarily faded. Here, too, the Jew found an effective, albeit unwitting, support in the venality of the official German policies of restricting the political education of the growing generations; and the result of this unholy combination was that the parliamentary plums, too, fell into the lap of the Jews.

So that in 1918 the Jews ruled in Germany in the offices of Government, State and Municipalities; they controlled finances, stock exchanges, and practically every business. The Universities and professions were overrun by them. What the Jews had in mind was insolently expressed by the Jewish-Austrian Minister of War "Deutsch", in an article by him; in "Kampf" he says, "Now, we Jews are on top now, we are the bosses! Our most glowing dreams have now come true."

We find the Jew in control of most department stores in Germany, of 50% of the real estate of Berlin, of 40% of the Restaurants and Coffee Houses, of shipping, theaters, newspapers, picture industry.

75% of all plays given on the German Stage were written by Jews, ably supported by the Society of German Theater Critics, the officers of which were Jews.

With the helps of the Jew-controlled press, the German masses learned to lean upon the radical political parties. These were controlled by the very Jews, who had benefited, at the expense of the Germans, from the shortsighted German Governmental policies, to which reference previously has been made.

Nevertheless, the simple-minded Germans never expected that the Jews, who came into power with the radical party tickets, would, with fiendish deliberation, not appoint Germans, but only Jews to every available political position, and would discharge, right and left, every German official they could from the offices of Government, States and Municipalities. They did this so thoroughly that soon no Government by Germans was left, and, just as thoroughly and true to Jewish tradition, there began a ruthless, unconscionable dissipation of funds until the various offices were bankrupted.

The conditions of government grew so chaotic that governing

had to be done by emergency decrees and by threats of dictatorship.

Because of these unbearable conditions, the adherents of the Monarchy hoped for a possible return of that regime. They might have been successful had they been able to advance satisfactory reasons why an Emperor, who under less trying conditions had failed to satisfactorily guide the ship of state, and finally had deserted it, should be more successful now when the problems of the country were infinitely more difficult to solve. The people could not be persuaded, they had lost confidence in the Monarchy, in right or left parties, of which there were 32! Indeed, they had lost confidence in the very possibility of a people to rule itself by parties; they had learned, by bitter experience, that it requires a leader to rule a people.

It is difficult to see why Wilhelm, with the help of his political and technical advisors and the excellent facilities available to him, could not have presented to the Germans a program that would conform with the best interests of the people and his own. It is evident that his sense of sportsmanship and liberality was not enough developed to lift him to that mediocre height.

One cannot escape the conclusion that the rank growth of the Jewish influence in Germany, which all but choked the German traditions, was encouraged by the Emperor, and his own selected advisors, who evidently did not share the sentiments expressed by Bismarck on this subject.

It was on June 15, 1847, in the Prussian Landtag, that Bismarck made the public confession that he shared the sentiment of the common people, of feeling ashamed of the company of Jews; that he could not conceive, of retaining his national self-respect and honor, were he compelled to pay obedience to a Jew. "I would not care," he continued, "to extend, nor would I want to see, a Jew occupy a position of authority in this state." That was plain enough for everyone to know where he stood, at that time.

Nevertheless, in 1873, Bismarck himself was taken in by the German Jewish Bankers. He wanted to establish a Central German Government Bank, but changed his mind, upon the advise of the Jewish Banker Bleichroeder, in favor of a Reichsbank under private control, to protect, so the Jew argued, the assets of the Reichsbank against the possibility of confiscation, in case of defeat in war. As result of this cunning suggestion, the control of the Reichsbank, monopoly of currency-issue, and privilege of coinage, fell into the hands of the Jews, the Reichsbank being controlled by eleven Jews and four Germans; probably Germans. Thus the Reichsbank, an institution whose importance is second only to the German Ministry of War, also fell into the hands of the Jews and gave them powers of such far-reaching importance the consequences of which but few Germans would be able to appreciate. Incidentally, the U.S. Federal Reserve Bank is similarly a private institution.

With this in mind, let us cast a look into the Emperors Ministry of War. We take for granted that this office carries an unparalleled responsibility for the protection of the country, its people and traditions, that it holds in the hollow of its hand every drop of German blood, and every single life in the Nation.

What were the reasons that soon after the outbreak of the War Jews began to filter into this desperately important citadel of Germany's defense? At a time when Germany was struggling for her very life, when it became more than ever before a measure of necessity that the dependability of its personnel be made humanly certain. There must have been a reason why Germans were displaced in the Ministry of War.

282 of the "down-trodden" race in the German Ministry of War! 282 descendants of Aaron, winning battle by holding up hands! 282 of the kind that can shake down the walls of Jericho by blowing of trumpets!

What Germans ever could have believed such a thing possible? Even Jewesses in the offices outnumbered their quota six to one, all this with no dearth of efficient German men and women. Israel looks after her own!

Was intimate contact with the Ministry of War valuable? What a question to ask?

Were there not important business contracts to be grabbed, patronage made available, Jewish soldiers to be protected against the hazards of the front, Jewish qualification for front service to be passed upon by Jewish physicians, of which there were plenty, officer-patents to be passed upon, distinctions and decorations to be distributed, and that we may not forget, information made available, obtainable only through intimate contact with the Ministry of War?

Instead of one to one hundred, the Jew was at the trough of business, finance, professions, at a rate of 60, 80, even 100 to 1, yet, whenever it meant physical labor, dangers to life and limb, he had the knack of knowing when and how to mysteriously melt away.

Israel looks after her own!

The German-Jews made it plain that their financial support of the war could be had only by advantages of this type, and so, everywhere the Jew was placed in a more favorable position, and even in a more favorable light than the ordinary German Kommiss at the front.

A chain is no stronger than its weakest link, and that weakest link of the German Government was her Jewish affiliations. The very existence of this link shows lack of traditional orientation expectable in those who look for protections, profit or pilfer, but damnable in those who were the trustees of Germany's heritage.

The summary which follows is based upon records of the German Ministry of War.

Total number of Germans in War service	12,500,000
Total number of Jews at front, including behind the lines, in offices, at telephones	21,455
Total number of Jews in the Commissary, in the Army of Occupation, at home, or serving without arms	40,817
German soldiers killed	1,500,000
Jewish soldiers killed	3,411
German active officers killed	12,500
Jewish active officers killed	78

```
Germans killed in relation to entire
population .......................................2.5%
Jews killed in relation to entire population ...........0.0055%
Decorations given to Germans, in relation to number
of Germans killed  .......................................1
Decorations given to Jews, in relation
to number of Jews killed  ................................6
Number of Jews at the front  ........................21,455
Decorations received by Jews  .......................21,601
In the form of Iron Crosses, First Class  ................900
Iron Crosses, Second Class  .........................17,000
Other decorations  ...................................3,701
```

To those who guided the destiny of Germany, the fact that the Jews hold the record for desertion from Military service had no meaning.

In Germany, between 1882 and 1892, 4,006 Jews deserted.

In 1916, the *Israelitische Familien Blatt* complains bitterly about England and France deporting to Russia 80,000 able-bodied Jews that had left Russia to escape military service.

The Russian General Martynor, in his book relating to the causes of the Russian Debacle in the Russo-Japanese War, says regarding the Jews: "From one division alone, 256 Jews deserted, as compared to 8 of other nationals. In 1914 five thousand able-bodied Jews arrived in Palestine, being deserters from the Russian Army. In 1910, of 20,000 Jews called to the colors in Russia 11,000 deserted."

I am convinced that were the Jew to fight under the flag of Israel, and within his own Jewish National Army, his record of desertion from the army would likely be the same as that of any other nationality.

In conclusion, reference is made to the beloved old Jewish philanthropist, Strauss, deceased. While crossing over on Staten Island, he exclaimed to a companion in reference to the Jews: "Ach, mine people, unless they mend their ways, and become good American citizens, in fact as well as in name, pogroms are coming to America, like no country has ever seen! I'm telling you!"

GERMANY FOR THE GERMANS

We are now coming to the less acute but more intrinsic causes of the hereditary German-Jewish conflict, causes the world as yet knows little about, for they lie further afield. We are living in a time of increasing consciousness. We have grown conscious of complexes, health, auto, radio, speed, even of the smell of our neighbor, for we have grown sanitary-conscious; but the German has grown acutely race-conscious. Unless the outsider can gauge the force that is behind this "Furor Germanicus," by sounding the traditional resources of the Germans of today, he cannot hope to understand this broader German problem, of which the Jewish problem is but an unimportant side issue.

Before the days of Darwin we were Bible and revival conscious, more pious than we are nowadays. We felt ourselves children alike of one God; we were taught to believe that we are born equal; taught to love our neighbor as ourselves, and to include every mother's son, be he Negro, Mongol, Jew or Gentile. It was hard to live up to this, but we did the best we could, to satisfy our conscience. We persuaded ourselves to love them one and all, but kept repairing the fence between our lot and the adjoining.

2000 years of such teaching has not stifled that still small voice within; 2000 years of professing brotherly love could not make us really feel it, could not bridge the chasm that separates man from man, and race from race, and eternally must.

It is the "voice of blood" within us; it is tradition! It is as Kipling says, "East is East and West is West, and never the twain shall meet."

This conflict between the demands of the blood and the demands of religion is the weak link in the human chain, the disturbing factor in humanity's equation. It enforces a mimicry of conduct which, be it tragical or comical, is always natural.

This inner struggle to unite and harmonize by argument and

persuasion, which for concrete racial reasons cannot be, and should not be, harmonized, leads to the disintegration of the racial consciousness, and is sapping the racial stamina of the Christian Nordic nations.

The Jew does not know, nor admit, he denies this sentimental equality; for him there are first Jews, then Gentiles. He is not suffering from this infernal internal soul conflict. The Jew has always been acutely race-conscious, while the national and religious history of, and the conflicts among, the Western Nordic nations indicate an appalling racial chaos.

For more than a thousand years the Christian Nordics drenched Europe's soil with the blood of their brothers, constantly decimating their own ranks, tens of millions killed alone in the late War. A strange something has been mixed with the Nordic blood, that creates this internal, never ending conflict. It is the blood and curse of an alien race within the Nordic's!

The Christian Western nations suffer from secularism in religion as well as in politics, which only the revival of the ancient Nordic traditions can cure.

During the 19th century our ideas were steeped in the Darwinian philosophy which, going Christianity one better, related man to all lower animals. In every nook and corner of science, philosophy and politics, there sat a Darwinian monkey. Darwinism has made us even monkey-conscious. Darwinism had a still further leveling effect upon social life, furnished plausible reasons for a purely materialistic viewpoint of life, it knocked from under us the last leg of our identity, our difference from other beings, it nourished in particular the radical mentality, it played into the hands of the Jews, as every disintegrating power seems to favor the Jews.

At the beginning of the 20th century Darwinism suddenly took a tumble. The simple sweetpea cross-breeding experiments of the German Catholic Priest, Mendel, has changed every social and racial concept. A thousand years may pass into history before a discovery of equal importance to the human race will likely be made.

The deductions drawn from these experiments have caused Germany to become highly conscious of the factors for good and evil that are at work within the blood and body of the Germanic as well as every other race.

"Racial standards" is the new key-word of Germany's policy. Germany has turned from an unsound, spreadeagle-nationalism, from a swanky militarism to a sound and unobtrusive nationalism.

Horticulturalists and stockbreeders have long ago applied the principles of true breeding, and established standards of purity of stock. Similarly, Germany knows today that any attempt at Germanizing alien blood is dynamiting her own. She knows that, solely within the Nordic blood stream can the Germanic soul manifest, that the assimilation of alien blood means growing a race of bastards. She cannot afford to ignore the experience of every breeder of stock.

Germany wants pure-bred Germans, not German-alien bastards. She will leave to Judah the breeding of true-bred Jews. That in short is the real issue involved, everything else is smoke.

This German-Jewish problem is painful to Jewry, bot because she is prevented from becoming assimilated, a thought furthest from her mind, but because she does not want to relinquish a profitable and advantageous field of her own peculiar activity, Germany culturally offers too much for Jewry to do without.

Germany is not opposed to Semites as such, she does not hate the Arabs and their culture, though Arabs are a true Semitic strain.

Germany is not so stupid as to think she could profit by atrocities, Jew-baiting or anti-Semitic rowdyism.

She has more important things to do, and prefers to pay attention to those that will hasten, and not retard, the realization of her policies. Germany has no need, nor desire, to imprint upon her escutcheon at this late date of history the fingerprints of murder or atrocity. The nobility of her tradition makes the very thought of "atrocities at Germany's behest" impossible to conceive.

Racial purity means more to her than immediate economic ad-

---

vantages. Economic advantages will be recovered in course of time. Germany is willing to sell her goods, but has no desire to sell her blood, nor buy that of an alien race, or have it forced upon her by threats of boycott.

She knows that every seed transmits the parental characteristics in plants and animals, as it does in humans. She does not want the alien characteristics in her race. She knows, inherited characteristics cannot be altered by any baptism, any belief, any training, any contact, any tradition, or any human effort.

Germany takes racial caste as an insurmountable reality. She realizes that racial characteristics must be protected, selected, cultivated, nursed. We do not allow a pure-bred female dog to run wild, if we do not want mongrels to jazz up the breed.

During the past some races ran wild, others protected themselves by rigid taboos. But taboos or none, a race cannot remain pure if it lives in every port of the world, and has no homeland in which to drive its roots.

Jazz is typically Jewish. Jazz takes what it finds and distorts character and beauty to suit the craze of the moment. Jazz is peculiarly parasitic and perverse. Today hardly anything is left that has not been jazzed up, government, public institutions, international relations, business, church, personality.

Germany is through with the "jazz of bastardization," through with Germanizing aliens.

She wants to build a new civilization of her own, to serve as a medium through which the German soul can give forth the best it holds. She insists upon the purity of the German racial structure, upon a bloodstream purged of alien strains.

Germany believes that an integrated racial structure is required for integrity of character and personality.

These are the reason why Germany is going to side-step the alien elements and why she insists upon removing especially the Jewish strain from her people.

This does not mean that Germany disrespects, or intends to dishonor, the Jewish race; to her the Jews are only one group of many aliens which she would just as rigidly exclude. To see an affront in this shows misunderstanding of the real issues involved.

Germany anticipates, and welcomes, a similar policy on the part of the Jews. She sees no reason why a pure-bred Jewish race should have less exalted ideals, and a less glorious future, than any other pure-bred race.

After the smoke of antagonism has cleared away, and Jewry has learned to see less passionately, and more clearly, she will bethink herself of her own peculiar racial greatness, and realize that this German-Jewish conflict has been a means to a closer knitting of the Jewish bonds, to a clarification of her own traditions. It is always the soul of the servant, the pariah, that is most easily offended. Noblesse oblige.

Accusations, defamations, insinuations and boycotts sink into insignificance in the presence of the nobility of life.

It is upon neutral ground that the German-Jewish question will properly and finally be settled.

Under the Swastika *was originally published before World War II by the Aryan Book Store, Los Angeles, California, and was reprinted in September of 1977 by, and additional copies are available from, Liberty Bell Publications.*

20 April 1889   **20 April 1989 — 68**   *30 April 1945*

ADOLF HITLER — 1889-1945

"It is necessary that I should die for my people; but my spirit will rise from the grave and the world will know that I was right."

HITLER SPEAKS TO AMERICA

Excerpts from *Mein Kampf*

Words of Guidance
to Lead Us Out of a Perilous Predicament

Preface

We are in a situation in America today analogous to that of the German people following Word War I. The Jews in America are in control of the media, finance, and the government. Pitilessly they are forcing the total integration of the White race with the black. Our representatives in government are mere puppets jerking about hither and yon on strings pulled by relentless Jewish puppeteers.

Confidence in the "American Way" has evaporated. White Americans no longer believe in the destiny of their country. They look for leadership, but the true leaders have been brought down by the Jews. What passes for leadership is a group of posturing political popinjays whose first concern is Israel, the second, their re-election.

Germany had the answer to such a predicament—a leader to lead them out of the abyss. We have no such leader, but we have

20 April 1889   **20 April 1989 — 69**   *30 April 1945*

the words of Adolf Hitler to lead us back toward higher ground until the true leader does appear.

This distillation of his thoughts in no way replaces the reading of *Mein Kampf* in its entirety. However, in this desperate hour the editor has selected some cogent paragraphs from this monumental work to show how applicable they are to our own time and distress. If anything, Adolf Hitler's mesage is even more applicable to the beleaguered Aryan race than it was in his own time to his own countrymen.

READ ON—AND BEGIN *THE MOVEMENT!*

THE MISSION OF THE NATION

from page 125

What we have to fight for is the necessary security for the existence and increase of our race and people, the subsistence of its children, and the maintenance of our racial stock unmixed, the freedom and independence of the Fatherland; so that our people may be enabled to fulfil the mission assigned to it by the Creator.

THE NEED FOR HIGHER IDEALS

from pages 213-214

By helping to lift the human being above the level of mere animal existence, Faith really contributes to consolidate and safeguard its own existence. Taking humanity as it exists today and taking into consideration the fact that the religious beliefs which it generally holds and which have been consolidated through our education, so that they serve as moral standards in practical life, if we should now abolish religious teaching and not replace it by anything of equal value, the result would be that the foundation of human existence would be seriously shaken. We may safely say that man does not live merely to serve higher ideals, but that these ideals, in their turn, furnish the necessary conditions of his existence as a human being. And thus the circle is closed.

WHAT THE SCHOOLS SHOULD TEACH

from pages 233-234

This is only one example among many. The deliberate training of fine and noble traits of character in our schools today is almost negative. In the future much more emphasis will have to be laid on this side of our educational work. Loyalty, self-sacrifice, and discretion are virtues which a great nation must possess. And the teaching and development of these in the school is a more important matter than many other things now included in the curriculum.

THE SMALL MINDS OF POLITICIANS

from page 123

Because of a certain vanity, which is always one of the blood-relations of unintelligence, the general run of politicians will always eschew those schemes for the future which are really difficult to put into practice; and they will practise this avoidance so that they may not lose the immediate favour of the mob. The importance and the success of such politicians belong exclusively to the present and will be of no consequence for the future. But that does not worry small-minded people; they are quite content with momentary results.

POLITICIANS CARE ONLY
ABOUT RE-ELECTION

from pages 210-211

Those people are always influenced by one and the same pre-occupation when they introduce something new into their programme and modify something already contained in it. That pre-occupation is directed towards the result of the next election. The moment these artists in paliamentary government have the first glimmering of a suspicion that their darling public may be ready to kick up its heels and escape from the harness of the old party wagon they begin to paint the shafts with new colours. On such occasions the party astrologers and horoscope readers, the so-called 'experienced men' and 'experts', come forward. For the most part they are old parliamentary hands whose political schooling has furnished them with ample experience. They can remember former occasions when the masses showed signs of losing patience and they now diagnose the menace of a similar situation arising. Resorting to their old prescription, they form a 'committee.' They go around among the darling public and listen to what is being said. They dip their noses into the newspapers and gradually begin to scent what it is that their darlings, the broad masses, are wishing for, what they reject and what they are hoping for. The groups that belong to each trade or business, and even office employees, are carefully studied and their innermost desires are investigated. The 'malicious slogans' of the opposition from which danger is threatened are now suddenly looked upon as worthy of reconsideration, and it often happens that these slogans, to the great astonishment of those who originally coined and circulated them, now appear to be quite harmless and indeed are to be found among the dogmas of the old parties.

When four years have passed, or in the meantime if there should be some critical weeks during which the parliamentary corporations have to face the danger of being dissolved, these honourable gentlemen become suddenly seized by an irresistible desire to act. Just as the grub-worm cannot help growing into a cockchafer, these parliamentarian worms leave the great House of Puppets and flutter on new wings out among the beloved public. They address the electors once again, give an account of the enormous labours they have accomplished and emphasize the malicious obstinacy of their opponents. They do not always meet with grateful applause; for occasionally the unintelligent masses throw rude and unfriendly remarks in their faces. When this spirit of public ingratitude reaches a certain pitch, there is only one way of saving the situation. The prestige of the party must be burnished up again. The programme has to be amended. The committee is called into existence once again. And the swindle begins anew. Once we understand the impenetrable stupidity of our public we cannot be surprised that such tactics turn out successful. Led by the Press and blinded once again by the alluring appearance of the new programme, the bourgeois as well as the proletarian herds of voters faithfully return to the common stall and re-elect their old deceivers. The 'people's man' and labour candidate now change back into the parliamentarian grub and become fat and rotund as they batten on the leaves that grow on the tree of public life – to be re-transformed into the glittering butterfly after another four years have passed.

THE INABILITY OF DEMOCRACY TO FIGHT COMMUNISM
from page 211-212

Scarcly anything else can be so depressing as to watch this process in sober reality and to be the eyewitness of this repeatedly recurring fraud. On a spiritual training ground of that kind it is not possible for the bourgeois forces to develop the strength which is necessary to carry on the fight against the organized might of Marxism. Indeed they have never seriously thought of doing so. Though these parliamentary quacks who represent the white race are generally recognized as persons of quite inferior mental capacity, they are shrewd enough to know that they could not seriously entertain the hope of being able to use the weapon of Western Democracy to fight a doctrine for the advance of which Western Democracy, with all its accessories, is employed as a means to an end. Democracy is exploited by the Marxists for the purpose of paralysing their opponents and gaining for themselves a free hand to put their own methods into action. When certain groups of Marxists use all their ingenuity for the time being to make it be believed that they are inseperably attached to the principles of democracy, it may be well to recall the fact that when critical occasions arose these same gentlemen snapped their fingers at the principle of decision by majority vote, as that principle is understood by Western Democracy.

THE INEQUALITY OF THE RACES

from pages 215-216

Over against all this, the *völkisch* concept of the world recognizes that the primordial racial elements are of the greatest significance for mankind. In principle, the State is looked upon only as a means to an end and this end is the conservation of the racial characteristics of mankind. Therefore on the *völkisch* principle we cannot admit that one race is equal to another. By recognizing that they are different, the *völkisch* concept separates mankind into races of superior and inferior quality. On the basis of this recognition it feels bound in conformity with the eternal Will that dominates the universe, to postulate the victory of the better and stronger and the subordination of the inferior and weaker. And so it pays homage to the truth that the principle underlying all Nature's operations is the aristocratic principle and it believes that this law holds good even down to the last individual organism. It selects individual values from the mass and thus operates as an organizing principle, whereas Marxism acts as a disintegrating solvent. The *völkisch* belief holds that humanity must have its ideals, because ideals are a necessary condition of human existence itself. But, on the other hand, it denies that an ethical ideal has the right to prevail if it endangers the existence of a race that is the standard-bearer of a higher ethical ideal. For in a world which would be composed of mongrels and negroids all ideals of human beauty and nobility and all hopes of an idealized future for our humanity would be lost for ever.

On this planet of ours human culture and civilization are indissolubly bound up with the presence of the Aryan. If he should be exterminated or subjugated, then the dark shroud of a new barbarian era would enfold the earth.

HOW THE JEW USES THE NEGRO TO BASTARDIZE THE WHITE RACE

from pages 184-185

The Jew uses every possible means to undermine the racial foundations of a subjugated people. In his systematic efforts to ruin girls and women he strives to break down the last barriers of discrimination between him and other peoples. The Jews were responsible for bringing negroes into the Rhineland, with the ultimate idea of bastardizing the white race which they hate and thus lowering its cultural and political level so that the Jew might dominate. For as long as a people remain racially pure and are conscious of the treasure of their blood, they can never be overcome by the Jew. Never in this world can the Jew become master of any people except a bastardized people.

This is why the Jew systematically endeavours to lower the racial quality of a people by permanently adulterating the blood of the individuals who make up that people.

HOW THE JEW KEEPS HIMSELF APART

from page 179

Even more watchfully than ever before, he now stood guard over his Jewish nationality. Though bubbling over with 'enlightenment,' 'progress,' 'liberty,' 'humanity,' etc., his first care was to preserve the racial integrity of his own people. He occasionally bestowed one of his female members on an influential Christian; but the racial stock of his male descendants was always preserved unmixed fundamentally. He poisons the blood of others but preserves his own blood unadulterated. The Jew scarcely ever marries a Christian girl, but the Christian takes a Jewess to wife. The mongrels that are a result of this latter union always declare themselves on the Jewish side. Thus a part of the higher nobility in particular became completely degenerate. The Jew was well aware of this fact and systematically used this means of disarming the intellectual leaders of the opposite race. To mask his tactics and fool his victims, he talks of the equality of all men, no matter what their race or colour may be. And the simpletons begin to believe him.

THE JEW ALWAYS REMAINS A JEW

from page 177

It is not however by the tie of language, and the Jew imself knows this better than any other, seeing that he attaches so little importance to the preservation of his own language while at the same time he strives his utmost to maintain his blood free from intermixture with that of other races. A man may acquire and use a new language without much trouble; but it is only his old ideas that he expresses through the new language. His inner nature is not modified thereby. The best proof of this is furnised by the Jew himself. He may speak a thousand tongues and yet his Jewish nature will remain always one and the same.

HOW THE JEW GAINS POWER

from page 175

(a) As soon as the first permanent settlements had been established the Jew was suddenly 'there.' He arrived as a merchant and in the beginning did not trouble to disguise his nationality. He still remained openly a Jew, partly it may be because he knew to little of the language. It may also be that people of other races refused to mix with him, so that he could not very well adopt any other appearance than that of a foreign merchant. Because of his subtlety and cunning and the lack of experience on the part of the people whose guest he became, it was not to his disadvantage openly to retain his Jewish character. This may even have been advantageous to him; for the foreigner was received kindly.

(b) Slowly but steadily he began to take part in the economic life around him; not as a producer, however, but only as a middleman. His commercial cunning, acquired through thousands of years of negotiation as an intermediary, made him superior in this field to the Aryans, who were still quite ingenuous and indeed clumsy and whose honesty was unlimited; so that after a short while commerce seemed destined to become a Jewish monopoly. The Jew began by lending out money at usurious interest, which is a permanent trade of his. It was he who first introduced the payment of interest on borrowed money. The danger which this innovation involved was not at first recognized; indeed the innovation was welcomed, because it offered momentary advantages.

(c) At this stage the Jew had become firmly settled down; that is to say, he inhabited special sections of the cities and towns and had his own quarter in the market-places. Thus he gradually came to form a State within a State. He came to look upon the commercial domain and all money transactions as a privilege belonging exclusively to himself and he exploited it ruthlessly.

(d) At this stage trade and finance had become his complete monopoly. Finally, his usurious rate of interest aroused opposition and the increasing impudence which the Jew began to manifest all round stirred up popular indignation, while his display of wealth gave rise to popular envy. The cup of his iniquity became full to the brim when he included landed property among his commercial wares and degraded the soil to the level of a market commodity. Since he himself never cultivated the soil but considered it as an object to be exploited, on which the peasant may still remain but only on condition that he submits to the most heartless exactions of his new master, public antipathy against the Jew steadily increased and finally turned into open animosity. His extortionate tyranny became so unbearable that people rebelled against his control and used physical violence against him. They began to scrutinize this foreigner somewhat more closely, and then began to discover the repulsive traits and characteristics inherent in him, until finally an abyss opened between the Jews and their hosts, across which abyss there could be no further contact.

In times of distress a wave of public anger has usually arisen against the Jew; the masses have taken the law into their own hands; they have seized Jewish property and ruined the Jew in their urge to protect themselves against what they consider to be a scourge of God. Having come to know the Jew intimately through the course of centuries, in times of distress they looked upon his presence among them as a public danger comparable to the plague.

(e) But then the Jew began to reveal his true character. He paid court to governments, with servile flattery, used his money to ingratiate himself further and thus regulary secured for himself once again the privilege of exploiting his victim. Although public wrath flared up against this eternal profiteer and drove him out, after a few years he reapeared in those same places and carried on as before. No persecution could force him to give up his trade of exploiting other people and no amount of harrying succeeded in driving him out permanently. He always returned after a short time and it was always the old story with him.

HOW THE JEW CONTROLS THE ECONOMY
from page 178

Yet at the same time he continued to undermine the groundwork of that part of the economic system in which the people have the most practical interest. He bought up stock in the various national undertakings and thus pushed his influence into the circuit of national production, making this latter an object of buying and selling on the stock exchange, or rather what might be called the pawn in a financial game of chess, and thus ruining the basis on which personal proprietorship alone is possible. Only with the entrance of the Jew did that feeling of estrangement between employers and employees begin which led at a later date to the political class struggle.

Finally the Jew gained an incresing influence in all economic undertakings by means of his predominance in the stock exchange. If not the ownership, at least he secured control of the working power of the nation.

HOW THE JEW USES AND CONTROLS THE PRESS

from page 58

In order to estimate properly the really pernicious influence which the Press can exercise one had to study this infamous Jewish method whereby honourable and decent people were besmirched with mud and filth, in the form of low abuse and slander, from hundreds and hundreds of quarters simultaneously, as if commanded by some magic formula.

These highway robbers would grab at anything which might serve their evil ends.

They would poke their noses into the most intimate family affairs and would not rest until they had sniffed out some petty item which could be used to destroy the reputation of their victim. But if the result of all this sniffing should be that nothing derogatory was discovered in the private or public life of the victim, they continued to hurl abuse at him, in the belief that some of their animadversions would stick even though refuted a thousand times. In most cases it finally turned out impossible for the victim to continue his defence, because the accuser worked together with so many accomplices that his slanders were re-echoed interminably. But these slanderers would never own that they were acting from motives which influence the common run of humanity or are understood by them. Oh, no. The scoundrel who defamed his contemporaries in this villainous way would crown himself with a halo of heroic probity fashioned of unctuous phraseology and twaddle about his 'duties as a Journalist' and other mouldy nonsense of that kind. When these cuttle-fishes gathered together in large shoals at meetings and congresses they would give out a lot of slimy talk about a special kind of honour which they called the professional honour of the journalist. Then the assembled species would bow their respects to one another.

THE JEW AND CIVIL RIGHTS

from page 177

Furthermore, his financial domination over all the spheres of economic life had become so powerful that he felt he could no longer sustain that enormous structure or add to it unless he were admitted to the full enjoyment of the 'rights of citizenship.' He aimed at both, preservation and expansion; for the higher he could climb the more alluring became the prospect of reaching the old goal, which was promised to him in ancient times, namely world-rulership, and which he now looked forward to with feverish eyes, as he thought he saw it visibly approaching. Therefore all his efforts were now directed to becoming a full-fledged citizen, endowed with all civil and political rights.

That was the reason for his emancipation from the Ghetto.

HOW THE JEW USES ZIONISM FOR WORLD DOMINATION

from page 184

(k) The Jewish domination in the States seems now so fully assured that not only can he now afford to call himself a Jew once again, but he even acknowledges freely and openly what his ideas are on racial and political questions. A section of the Jews avows itself quite openly as an alien people, but even here there is another falsehood. When the Zionists try to make the rest of the world believe that the new national consciousness of the Jews will be satisfied by the establishment of a Jewish State in Palestine, the Jews thereby adopt another means to dupe the simpleminded Gentile. They have not the slightest intention of building up a Jewish State in Palestine so as to live in it. What they really are aiming at is to establish a central organization for their international swindling and cheating. As a sovereign State, this cannot be controlled by any of the other States. Therefore it can serve as a refuge for swindlers who have been found out and at the same time a highschool for the training of other swindlers.

THE JEW AS CULTURE-DESTROYER

from page 185

Culturally his activity consists of bowdlerizing art, literature and the theatre, holding the expressions of national sentiment up to scorn, overturning all concepts of the sublime and beautiful, the worthy and the good, finally dragging the people to the level of his own low mentality.

Of religion he makes a mockery. Morality and decency are described as antiquated prejudices and thus a systematic attack is made to undermine those last foundations on which the national being must rest if the nation is to struggle for its existence in this world.

HOW THE JEW DESTROYS THE NATION

from page 185

Economically he brings about the destruction of the State by a systematic method of sabotaging social enterprises until these become so costly that they are taken out of the hands of the State and then submitted to the control of Jewish finance. Politically he works to withdraw from the State its means of subsistence, inasmuch as he undermines the foundations of national resistance and defence, destroys the confidence which the people have in their Government, reviles the past and its history and drags everything national down into the gutter.

(l) Now begins the great and final revolution. As soon as the Jew is in possession of political power he drops the last few veils which have hitherto helped to conceal his features. Out of the democratic Jew, the Jew of the People, arises the 'Jew of the Blood,' the tyrant of the peoples. In the course of a few years he endeavours to exterminate all those who represent the national intelligence. And by thus depriving the peoples of their natural intellectual leaders he fits them for their fate as slaves under a lasting despotism.

Russia furnishes the most terrible example of such a slavery. In that country the Jew killed or starved thirty millions of people, in a bout of savage fanaticism and partly by the employment of inhuman torture. And he did this so that a gang of Jewish literati and financial bandits should dominate over a great people.

But the final consequence is not merely that the people lose all their freedom under the domination of the Jews, but that in the end these parasites themselves disappear. The death of the victim is followed sooner or later by that of the vampire.

HOW TO FORM A MOVEMENT TO REGAIN THE NATION

from page 195

(9) The nature and internal organization of the new movement make it anti-parliamentarian. That is to say, it rejects in general and in its own structure all those principles according to which decisions are to be taken on the vote of the majority and according to which the leader is only the executor of the will and opinion of others. The movement lays down the principle that, in the smallest as well as in the greatest problems, one person must have absolute authority and bear all responsibility.

THE PRACTICAL CONSEQUENCES OF THIS PRINCIPLE IN THE MOVEMENT

from page 195

In our movement the practical consequences of this principle are the following:

The president of a large group is appointed by the head of the group immediately above his in authority. He is then the responsible leader of his group. All the committees are subject to his authority and not he to theirs. There is no such thing as committees that vote but only committees that work. This work is allotted by the responsible leader, who is the president of the group. The same principle applies to the higher organizations—the *Bezirk* (district), the *Kreis* (urban circuit) and the *Gau* (the region). In each case the president is appointed from above and is invested with full authority and executive power. Only the leader of the whole party is elected at the general meeting of the members. But he is the sole leader of the movement. All the committees are responsible to him, but he is not responsible to the committees. His decision if final, but he bears the whole responsibility of it.

THE HEAVY RESPONSIBILITY OF THE LEADER

from page 196

The man who becomes leader is invested with the highest and unlimited authority, but he also has to bear the last and gravest responsibility.

The man who has not the courage to shoulder responsibility for his actions is not fitted to be a leader. Only a man of heroic mould can have the vocation for such a task.

Human progress and human cultures are not founded by the multitude. They are exclusively the work of personal genius and personal efficiency.

THE QUALITIES OF LEADERSHIP

from page 198

The will to be a leader is not a sufficient qualification for leadership. For the leader must have the other necessary qualities. Among these qualities will-power and energy must be considered as more serviceable than the intellect of a genius. The most valuable association of qualities is to be found in a combination of talent, determination and perseverance.

THE GROWTH OF THE MOVEMENT THROUGH THE LEADER

from page 196-197

A creative idea takes shape in the mind of somebody who thereupon feels himself called upon to transmit this idea to the world. He propounds his faith before others and thereby gradually wins a certain number of followers. This direct and personal way of promulgating one's ideas among one's contemporaries is the most natural and the most ideal. But as the movement develops and secures a large number of followers it gradually becomes impossible for the original founder of the doctrine on which the movement is based to carry on his propaganda personally among his innumerable followers and at the same time guide the course of the movement.

According as the community of followers increases, direct communication between the head and the individual followers becomes impossible. This intercourse must then take place through an intermediary apparatus introduced into the framework of the movement. Thus ideal conditions of inter-communication cease, and organization has to be introduced as a necessary evil. Small subsidiary groups come into existence, as in the political movement, for example, where the local groups represent the germ-cells out of which the organization develops later on.

THE IMPORTANCE OF A FOCAL CENTER IN THE MOVEMENT

from page 197

But such sub-divisions must not be introduced into the movement until the authority of the spiritual founder and of the school he has created are accepted without reservation. Otherwise the movement would run the risk of becoming split up by divergent doctrines. In this connection too much emphasis cannot be laid on the importance of having one geographic centre as the chief seat of the movement. Only the existence of such a seat or centre, around which a magic charm such as that of Mecca or Rome is woven, can supply a movement with that permanent driving force which has its source in the internal unity of the movement and the recognition of one head as representing this unity.

When the first germinal cells of the organization are being formed care must always be taken to insist on the importance of the place where the idea originated. The creative, moral and practical greatness of the place whence the movement went forth and from which it is governed must be exalted to a supreme symbol, and this must be honoured all the more according as the original cells of the movement become so numerous that they have to be regrouped into larger units in the structure of the organization.

THE PRINCIPLE OF STRUGGLE IN THE MOVEMENT

from page 199

A movement can become great only if the unhampered development of its internal strength be safeguarded and steadfastly augmented, until victory of all its competitors be secured.

One may safely say that the strength of a movement and its right to existence can be developed only as long as it remains true to the principle that struggle is a necessary condition of its progress and that its maximum strength will be reached only as soon as complete victory has been won.

Therefore a movement must not strive to obtain successes that will be only immediate and transitory, but it must show a spirit of uncompromising perseverance in carrying through a long struggle which will secure for it a long period of inner growth.

HOW THE JEW WILL ATTACK THE MOVEMENT

from page 199-200

The followers of the movement, and indeed the whole nation,

must be reminded again and again of the fact that, through the medium of his newspapers, the Jew is always spreading falsehood and that if he tells the truth on some occasions it is only for the purpose of masking some greater deceit, which turns the apparent truth into a deliberate falsehood. The Jew is the Great Master of Lies. Falsehood and duplicity are the weapons with which he fights.

Every calumny and falsehood published by the Jews are tokens of honour which can be worn by our comrades. He whom they decry most is nearest to our hearts and he whom they mortally hate is our best friend.

If a comrade of ours opens a Jewish newspaper in the morning and does not find himself vilified there, then he has spent yesterday to no account. For if he had achieved something he would be persecuted, slandered, derided and abused. Those who effectively combat this mortal enemy of our people, who is at the same time the enemy of all Aryan peoples and all culture, can only expect to arouse opposition on the part of his race and become the object of its slanderous attacks.

VENERATE THE LEADER AND FEAR NOT THE JEWS

from page 200

The greatest revolutions and the greatest achievements of this world, its greatest cultural works and the immortal creations of great statesmen, are inseparably bound up with one name which stands as a symbol for them in each respective case. The failure to pay tribute to one of those great spirits signifies a neglect of that enormous source of power which lies in the remembrance of all great men and women.

The Jew himself knows this best. He, whose great men have always been great only in their efforts to destroy mankind and its civilization, takes good care that they are worshipped as idols. But the Jew tries to degrade the honour in which nations hold their great men' and women. He stigmatizes this honour as the 'cult of personality.'

As soon as a nation has so far lost its courage as to submit to this impudent defamation on the part of the Jews it renounces the most important source of its own inner strength. The inner force cannot rise from a policy of pandering to the masses but only from the worship of men of genius, whose lives have uplifted and ennobled the nation itself.

When men's hearts are breaking and their souls are plunged into the depths of despair, their great forbears turn their eyes towards them from the dim shadows of the past — those forbears who knew how to triumph over anxiety and affliction, mental servitude and physical bondage — and extend their eternal hands in a gesture of encouragement to despairing souls. Woe to the nation that is ashamed to clasp those hands.

EPILOGUE
from page 378

ON NOVEMBER 9TH, 1923, FOUR AND A HALF YEARS AFTER ITS FOUNDATION, the German National Socialist Labour Party was dissolved and forbidden throughout the whole of the Reich. Today, in November 1926, it is again established throughout the Reich, enjoying full liberty, stronger and internally more compact than ever before.

All persecutions of the Movement and the individuals at its head, all the imputations and calumnis, have not been able to prevail against it. Thanks to the justice of its ideas, the integrity of its intentions and the spirit of self-denial that animates its members, it has overcome all oppression and increased its strength through the ordeal. If, in our contemporary world of parliamentary corruption, our Movement remains always conscious of the profound nature of its struggle and feels that it personifies the values of individual personality and race, and orders its action accordingly — then it may count with mathematical certainty on achieving victory some day in the future. And Germany must necessarily win the position which belongs to it on this Earth if it is led and organized according to these principles.

A State which, in an epoch of racial adulteration, devotes itself to the duty of preserving the best elements of its racial stock must one day become ruler of the Earth.

The adherents of our Movement must always remember this, whenever they may have misgivings lest the greatness of the sacrifices demanded of them may not be justified by the possibilities of success.

All quotes from the unexpurgated edition, of Mein Kampf, translated and annotated by James Murphy, first published on 21 March 1939 by Hurst and Blackett, Ltd., London, New York, Melbourne, and available at $10.00 + $1.50 for postage/handling for the paperback edition (Ord. No. 01001); $14.00 + $2.00 for the hardback edition (Ord. No. 01002). A German-language, hardback reprint of the 1943 edition (Ord. No. 38062) is available at $35.00 + $3.00 for postage/handling. Order from Liberty Bell Publications, Box 21, Reedy WV 25270 USA.

Sächsische Jugend huldigt dem Führer in Leipzig, 1933

20 April 1889   **20 April 1989 — 88**   *30 April 1945*

THE TRUTH ABOUT THE
BIG LIE

Everybody has heard about the "Big-Lie" propaganda technique. American newspapers often refer to it as "Hitler's big-lie
technique." The idea is that the more brazen and arrogant a liar is,
the less likely he is to get caught. We've been told over and over
again that this was a favorite "Nazi" propaganda trick and that
Adolf Hitler was the one who was primarily responsible for it.

The most prominent and "respectable" Jewish propaganda organization in America, the Anti-Defamation League of B'nai B'rith,
has published a pamphlet on National Socialism, a portion of which
is photographically reproduced below:

the Anatomy
of Nazism

Published by:

The Anti-Defamation League of B'nai B'rith
515 Madison Avenue, New York 22, N. Y.

in cooperation with

The Free Sons of Israel • 257 West 93rd Street, New York 25,

Of course, part of the Nazi propaganda technique was simply the
art of fabrication. Hitler wrote: "A definite factor in getting a lie
believed is the size of the lie. The broad mass of the people, in the
simplicity of their hearts, more easily fall victim to a big lie than to
a small one."

Before Austria was invaded, Hitler said publicly. "The annexa...

20 April 1889   *20 April 1989 – 89*   *30 April 1945*

You can get a copy of this pamphlet yourself by sending fifty cents to the ADL office in New York. Notice in the excerpt above that the pamphlet quotes from *Mein Kampf* to "prove" that Hitler advocated the "big-lie." Now read below what Adolf Hitler *really* said about the "big-lie." You can check this for yourself too. The following excerpts are from page 232 of the English translation of *Mein Kampf* which the Houghton-Mifflin Co. is selling:

It required the whole bottomless falsehood of the Jews and their Marxist fighting organization to lay the blame for the collapse on that very man who alone, with superhuman energy and will power, tried to prevent the catastrophe he foresaw and save the nation from its time of deepest humiliation and disgrace. By branding Ludendorff as guilty for the loss of the World War [WW I], they took the weapon of moral right from the one dangerous accuser who could have risen against the traitors to the fatherland. In this they proceeded on the sound principle that the magnitude of a lie always contains a certain factor of credibility, since the great masses of the people in the very bottom of their hearts tend to be corrupted rather than consciously and purposely evil, and that, therefore, in view of the primitive simplicity of their minds, they more easily fall a victim to a big lie than to a little one, since they themselves lie in little things, but would be ashamed of lies that were too big. Such a falsehood will never enter their heads, and they will not be able to believe in the possibility of such monstrous effrontery and infamous misrepresentation in others; yes, even when enlightened on the subject, they will long doubt and waver, and continue to accept at least one of these causes as true. Therefore, something of even the most insolent lie will always remain and stick—a fact which all 'the great lie-virtuosi and lying-clubs in this world know only too well and also make the most treacherous use of.

The foremost connoisseurs of this truth regarding the posibilities in the use of falsehood and slander have always been the Jews; for after all, their whole existence is based on one single great lie, to wit, that they are a religious community while actually they are a race—and what a race! One of the greatest minds of humanity has nailed them forever as such in an eternally correct phrase of fundamental truth: he called them 'the great masters of lie.' And anyone who does not recognize this or does not want to believe it will never in this world be able to help the truth to victory.

Now you can plainly see that the Jews have deliberately misrepresented to you what Adolf Hitler said. Hitler's own attitude toward the "big-lie" was crystal clear: he thoroughly deplored its use and pinned its origin solidly on the Jews themselves. And the Jews responded to this accusation in typical fashion—with another "big-lie," brazenly attempting to distort Hitler's meaning in their pamphlet, as you have seen.

Nor is this arrogant mendacity confined to the Jews in the Anti-Defamation League. As we mentioned, Jewish editors and newspaper writers have waged a major campaign for decades attempting to hide their own guilt by accusing National Socialists of advocating the "big-lie."

You don't have to drink a whole quart of sour milk to know it is sour. And when you find a man who tells you a whopping lie, you don't have to investigate everything else he tells you to know he is a liar.

The fact is that the Jews, as a group, have long had a deliberate policy of lying to non-Jewish Americans. They lied to us about Hitler and about National Socialist Germany, because they wanted America to go to war with Hitler.

They have lied to us about their own role in setting up the Communist conspiracy, which has spread out from Russia until it has engulfed half the earth and consumed tens of millions of human lives.

They have lied to us about the facts of race, because they want to bring about massive Negro-White racial intermixture in America.

And they have lied to us about a great number of other things too [including their most infamous scheme: the so-called "Holocaust"].

Reprinted from a pamphlet originally published by the National Socialist White People's Party [now known as The New Order], P.O. Box 27486,Milwaukee WI 53227.

Ehret die Arbeit und achtet den Arbeiter

ADOLF HITLER

HITLER, THE WORKLESS
AND THE NEEDY

In the autumn of his first year as Chancellor Adolf Hitler issued what was at once an order and an announcement, "This winter no one must starve or freeze in Germany."

Lots of people scarcely took the words for sober ernest, they saw no possibility of them being made good. Indeed how should this state of things be realised; the burdens and deprivations of the late War [WW I] still weighed heavily on all the world; never had it been possible hitherto that people should neither starve nor freeze to death in winter!

One might safely say that such an ideal never would have been practicable, had not a man directed affairs in Germany who knew how to bring into the sphere of practical politics that simple Christian charity one to another which the churches have been preaching throughout the ages.

Hitler's motto had long been "Love your neighbor *more* than yourself. Be ready, always, for the least of your own, to sacrifice your belongings and your life." It is known, of course, that Hitler accepts no income from his Chancellorship, but directs that this money should go towards the relief of unemployment. It may not equally well be known that during the winter 1933-34, when the sales of his book had reached the peak, the whole of this incre-

---

20 April 1889   **20 April 1989 — 92**   *30 April 1945*

ment was also ear-marked for the poor.

The Germans have a special gift for organisation. Hence it seemed eminently practical to organise the "Winter Relief Work" (Winterhilfswerk) by means of the Party machine. It was extraordinary to see how everybody took advantage of this to bring his own, personal sacrifice and exertions into line with the Führer's design and behest. No fewer than one and a half million people of position and influence threw themselves whole-heartedly into this great effort, to say nothing of the rank and file who also did their utmost, and of those who willingly gave their mite.

The scope of this, the biggest philanthropic effort ever made at one time by one people, was so all-embracing that, enlisting as it did the co-operation of great and small alike, it would require three times as much space at our command, merely to outline it. Some idea of it, however, we must endeavour to convey for three reasons, first to combat the often repeated gibe that Adolf Hitler has no constructive ability, no seizable plans; second, to show—if it really should need showing—how and why it is that he holds the trust and love of the German people as a whole; and thirdly, to claim for him that he lost no time at all after coming to power, in proceeding to make good the promises of his Party programme.

(Since the bulk of this book is, after all, to be limited, it may be that but little space will remain for even the slightest sketch of what more—in a dozen directions—Adolf Hitler has already done under this third heading. Every one of the social enterprises he has undertaken for the amelioration of living conditions and lack-of-outlook in Germany, would require a chapter in itself.

In no smallest village in Germany, nay, in no poorest cot was something not done, something not spared, to aid this nation-wide work. It was generally estimated that some three hundred million marks were devoted to it in this way. Possibly this estimate is too low. Not, by any means, that the Winterhilfsarbeit (Winter-aid-work) could merely be measured in terms of money. Nor could it be measured in terms of material comfort. Its value for the union and solidarity of the reawakened German spirit was above all these.

Given, then, this fount of money, let us very briefly enumerate the numerous channels into which its flow was directed.

Adolf Hitler called upon everyone who had a job of any sort, big or small, to set aside weekly or monthly some small saving for the poor. It was a request, not an order, for Hitler knew well enough that very many people were in no position to spare a single pfennig (fifth part of a penny). All who possibly could, came forward with their "bit" for the "Battle with Hunger and Cold." The directors of the whole enterprise set it an excellent example, and the rank and file willingly proved their Socialism in response.

Every Sunday during that whole winter hundreds and thousands of collectors were to be seen selling tags in the street to the same end.

Through this source alone enormous sums were gathered in, and very often other results came from these tag days. Case after case occurred of their leading to employment for the unemployed. For instance, in the Harz Mountains in Thuringia there are little towns whose inhabitants live by glass blowing. At this time unemployment was rife among them. So the directors of the Winter-Aid thought it a good thing to have tags made of glass, and gave this welcome order throughout the district. It resulted in months of work for three thousand poor glass workers in Thuringia.

The whole "brain wave" was so much appreciated by the public that when these glass tags appeared upon the streets there was a rush for them. In three days over twenty-five million were sold out! Could any better proof be adduced than this of how truly National Socialism concerns itself with the needs of even the smallest of the German workers?

Dr. Goebbels, one of the most genial and versatile of the men round Hitler, did not fail to bring his bright wits to bear upon the problems of the Winter-Aid. He it was who conceived the idea of the "Eintopfgericht" — the One-Pot-Dinner. Every German, especially everyone blessed with a decent share of this world's goods, was invited throughout the winter on the first Sunday of every month to restrict his main meal to extremely modest (financial) limits, to not more than about 6d., but to give over to a collector, who would call for it next day, the money which would otherwise have been laid out to furnish the table in the ordinary way. It was as if an Englishman saved what he would have spent on his "cut-from-the-joint and two vegs," (to say nothing of sweets and coffee), and gave it away and contented himself with — what shall we say? — one good old plate of hash or soup instead, and *nothing but soup.*

All the restaurants and hotels were advised to offer on their menus for that first Sunday nothing but this one-dish-dinner, but to charge for it according to usual *table d'hôte* or *à la carte* meals. The difference, of course, was to be handed over for the Winter-Aid. The success of this original idea was enormous. Like one man the whole people took it up. The venerable President himself ate a one-dish dinner on the first Sunday of every month.

During the winter over twenty million marks came to hand this way. Again, in this instance, the good of it was not confined to mere material things. The poor saw the Better-off willingly depriving themselves to help them, and the impression it made was of the best for the conception of "national-socialism." Dr. Goebbels hit on the happy slogan: "Don't spend: deny yourself." This went even further. When a rich man gets up from a well-spread table, and gives something to the poor, it is good, but it is not a sacrifice. The sacrifice comes in when a man contents himself with a poor meal instead of a better one, for the sake of giving something away to the man who never feeds well.

Then again — here was a splendid notion! Very often during that winter there was to be heard a cheerful bugling in the streets, and there was to be seen a truckload of soldiers slowly tooling by, blowing for all they were worth. What was this? Why — rummage collecting for the needy. Whenever a hand waved, or a door opened, or someone beckoned from window or corner, the truck hastened up, a couple of men leaped down and ran to obey the summons.

Most people had something they could do without for the Winter-Aid. Here it was an old sofa, — quickly handled and bestowed, — here a sewing machine — swung up atop — here chairs needing mending, here a bundle of clothes, here oddments for repairs of all sorts, here crockery, here spare pots or pans — up and down the streets went the truck, fanfaronading everywhere, and loading up cheerfully and dexterously like a furniture van!

Then workrooms were opened for necessitous girls and women, where these second-hand things could be made over, in return for groceries and shoes.

The happiest Christmas Germany had celebrated for many a long year was the first Christmas of Hitler's Chancellorship. It was the first Christmas after these so-called heathen Nazis had come to power. Up to this time Christmas in Germany had largely been a purely family affair. The tens of thousands of those who had no family, no relatives, no home, perhaps, merely looked on from afar.

Such a thing as this had to be put a stop to in the National Socialist State. On Christmas Eve the Party set up, at its own expense, great Christmas trees before many of the church doors, and in many of the open spaces in the cities. These were all aglitter with frost, and burning candles. Tables were spread beneath them. And bands played the immemorial hymns and carols of the season. Speeches were made calling upon those who were keeping up the feast at home, to remember their poorest brethren without, and to show them the good comradeship and brotherliness which was the very essence of National Socialism. This exhortation closed everywhere with the carol "Stille Nacht, Heilige Nacht."

Then came the crush — the rush — the stampede to the tables where hundreds of good folk forced their way to lay their gifts and offerings and contributions and goodies for the poor. Mountains of these things piled up until there wasn't an inch of room left to bestow a single gift more. Even the ground under the table and all around was cluttered with presents. When the donors had really done, and were ready to go back home again, these things were distributed to the lonely and the hungry and the friendless who gladly came forward to receive them. In ways like this National Socialism sought to prove itself not merely a political creed but a practical befriending of the people.

The Winter-Aid was signally supported by peasants, tradespeople and all sorts of industries, whose carts and waggons were daily to be seen in long rows at the doors of the offices of the Organisation, unloading goods and comestibles for the poor. No end of vouchers were issued by means of which the poor could obtain the necessaries of existence without having to expend money. So far as statistics can give any idea of what this amounted to – and statistics take no account of the Christmas presents – the following figures tell their own tale:

```
Expended –
Coals, about ............................... 2,600,000 tons
worth .................................... 50,000,000 marks.
Potatoes ................................... 12,500,000 cwt.
Vegetables & Flour ......................... 1,100,000 cwt.
Bread ........................................ 60,000 cwt.
Tinned Goods .............................. 300,000 tins.
Milk ...................................... 1,000,000 litres.
Shoes ...................................... 180,000 pairs.
Cloth ...................................... 250,000 metres.
Garments ...................................... 1,100,000.
Wood ........................................ 300,000 cwt.
Vouchers .................................... 400,000 marks.
Cash ...................................... 75,000,000 marks,
part of it from the One-Dish Dinner source.
```

The Foodstuff were not always distributed uncooked, but prepared in common kitchens, so that for the equivalent of an English twopence a hungry man could come by a real good meal. In Munich (Population *c.* 750,000) alone that winter daily portions were served from fifteen great communal kitchens to no less than three thousand poor people. Seventeen millions of unemployed, casual labourers, widows and orphans were supported through these efforts of the people as a whole.

It was a tough struggle to do it. But it was the wish of the Führer that this great work should be put in hand, that no one in Germany should starve or freeze, and everyone rejoiced to help in its fulfilment. While everywhere else in Europe the melancholy spectacle was only too often to be witnessed of hunger marchers parading the streets, of the workless and the despairing losing all patience and breaking out into strife and bitter class hatred, in Germany at least Adolf Hitler had united everyone in an unparalleled gesture of fraternal charity.

MOTHER AND CHILD

The winter passed. But the gigantic machinery of its Aid work remained, and Hitler, who could know no rest until he had given every possible demonstration of what National Socialism meant translated into terms of every-day life — Hitler looked round for the next immediate use to which it could be put.

He was already grappling with the problem of unemployment, and now he turned from the consideration of the father of the family, to that of the mother. This matter of maternity and infant welfare had long been comprised in the Party programme under the heading "It is the duty of the State to ensure the health of the people through due care bestowed upon mothers and children."

So work was immediately set on foot to relieve the terrible burdens weighing so heavily upon the poorer families of the land, and especially upon the toiling housewives. The War and its long subsequent list of privations and bitter hardships had told on this most helpless and defenceless portion of the community as heavily as on every other. This new movement in aid of womankind was at once a recognition of the bravery and suffering of the women of the terrible years gone by, and a beacon of hope for the nameless regiment of brave and struggling women of the present time.

First of all, the "Mother-and-Child" Movement undertakes to unearth hidden and secret misery (in order to relieve it), to explore special areas of distress, and to do away with red tape and mistaken economies. The whole thing is to turn upon the personal and individual touch. First the mother of the family is to be supported and helped and then every one of those dependent upon her. The Mother-and-Child work sets itself very few limits.

Needless to say, here again the scope of the enterprise is so wide only the briefest description of it can be given.

The greatest necessity — that of nourishment — calls for the first attention. Better food is to be provided, and sufficient milk for the children. Then comes the question of clothing and adequate laundry facilities. Women with big families swarming around them all day are to receive daily outside help.

The work of the "Arbeitsplatzhilfe" — roughly translated "The Job Finding Agency" — concerns itself largely with placing out the elder children of these numerous broods in suitable posts as soon as they are fit to earn, and help themselves. The hitherto earning mothers of these families are to be enabled at once to leave factory or business and return home where their duty and their most important work obviously lies. The *man* it is who must be enabled to go out and work and keep the home. Through the "Wohnungshilfe" (Dwelling-house Aid), a mighty attempt is to be made to sweep away the slums and miserable areas in great cities. Either such dwellings as already exist are to be improved and repaired, or entirely pulled down and rebuilt. Property owners who allow their houses to fall into bad condition are to be called to account for it. The unsocial attitude of those who decline to let where there are children is to be sharply corrected.

The Mother-and-Child Aid looks to it that poor families should have at least what furniture is barely necessary, especially beds. A special activity has been set on foot all through Germany whose slogan is "To each child his own bed." And these beds are collected from charitable donors in the same way as similar collections were made from house to house in the winter by the truckloads of trumpet-blowing soldiers.

Another branch of this work is to provide at least four weeks' country holiday or convalescence for mothers who stand in special need of rest and recuperation. The children are meantime to be cared for in kindergarten. For that short space, at least, the mother is to be wholly free. The home, during the interval, is to be kept going by means of the "Frauenarbeitsdienst" — the organisation which provides women's work of this kind for just these purposes, so that the husband and father can go on having his meals as usual, without universal domestic upset, just because the main prop and stay of it all — the wife and mother — has had to go away.

Then there are schools for mothers; many of these are run by doctors who make it their business to impart all sorts of essential information about food and health in general to these poor women. They can always resort to medical advice without fear or hesitation, since nothing is more important to a nation than its mothers, its children and its health.

All these measures, these undertakings, these departures and these immediate practicalities spring from the text laid down in *Mein Kampf*, the text is ruthlessly worked out in the life story of the Führer himself, "Social work must be tackled from below, not from above."

UNEMPLOYMENT

"We hold it to be the prime duty of the State to see that the citizen can secure means of livelihood."

Here, once more, we have one of the most important statements of Party undertakings. Hitler has held it of primary importance to combat unemployment by every permissible means devisable by ingenuity and ardent purpose.

This nation-wide struggle postulates immense governmental preparations. It is not one to be tackled piecemeal and by temporary measures. The whole reconstruction is to be built up after Hitler's own scheme and recommendations, schemes which embrace every sphere of industry, of private and public life. Not a struggle merely, but indeed, a mighty campaign against unemployment has been launched in Germany. It is hoped at last to obtain the victory over decades-long misery and ever-recurring industrial crises. Every man in the country must bear his part in this gigantic enterprise. The victory means nothing less than a stable recovery of industry. A strong State is the guarantor of steady business. Every possible means has been co-ordinated to this end.

The state has provided the sinews of war for this struggle, but the German people themselves have also subscribed many millions of marks for the promotion of national industry. In 1933 the Government set aside 4.3 milliards (4,300,000,000 Reichsmark), in 1934 about 5 milliards to finance schemes of work for the unemployed.

Vast plans were put in hand for the making of canals, for the building of power plants. Nearly all the greater rivers of Germany were harnessed to some productive purpose. By the expenditure of one hundred million marks, one million workmen could be kept employed for an entire month. The work on the Weser, and on the Dortmund-Ems Canal will keep twenty thousand men in work for four years. Another gigantic canal, begun in 1933 will provide work for 1,510,000 days. In the same district between Hannover and Magdeburg one hundred and ten square miles will be brought into cultivation which have hitherto been mere waste or swamp. In order to secure more land for husbandry in Schleswig-Holstein, two great dams are to be constructed across the Elbe River. The work will last three years. Thousands will thereby support themselves, and a plain of 225 square miles will be reclaimed. The enterprise can well be compared with that of Signor Mussolini on the Pontine Marshes.

The German Government offers to meet 40 per cent of the cost to everyone who builds a house or who proposes to carry out reparations and improvements. The result of this step is scarcely to be believed. The building trade, hitherto at a very low ebb, has looked up and gone ahead surprisingly. And consequently so have all the allied industries. Factories are at work day and night. In the spring of 1934 in many large German cities not a single skilled man in the building trade was out of work. This flourishing state of affairs repercussed on the machine industry and gave work to again another ten thousand men. Hitler, himself an ardent motor mechanic, has found the way for a vast revival in the motor-car industry by reducing the tax. The number of cars on the road doubled in 1933. One can judge of the cheerful position of affairs in this direction from the assurances made by motor-car manufacturers that they are in a position to deliver the goods at once.

The most important attack on unemployment, however, was delivered when the building of immense new arterial roads [the famous Autobahn. — *Editor*] was planned on the direct initiative of the Chancellor. This constitutes the biggest thing ever done yet in this direction. From four to five thousand miles of auto-roads are projected to be built in six directions right across the country. Two will run from north to south, one from Kiel via Hamburg, Bremen, the Schwarzwald to Basle, the other from East Prussia via Berlin and Munich to the Alps. Three of these great roads will run from east to west, one from Frankfurt-Oder, and the other from Breslau to the Rheinland, and one from Saarbrücken to Salzburg. This last one is to be called the Nibelungen Road. The sixth of the whole series will run from Hamburg to Breslau. All these roads will be built on the most modern lines.

They will be practically all on one grade and in no way interrupted by crossings. Other roads will be carried over by bridges. The entire plan will require many years to carry out. The Government has earmarked over two milliards of marks a year towards it. Whole armies of men find employment on it. The project is a proud one, for it not only resembles the great engineering feats of the Romans, but promises to change the face of the entire country for coming generations.

These are the ideas of young leaders confided to the might and craft of young workers to carry out, all working together to reduce — and ultimately to extinguish — the hideous curse of Unemployment in Germany.

WORK CAMPS

The idea of the Work Camp (which was originally envisaged on volunteer lines, students alone being obliged to attend), also proposed fruitful means of combatting unemployment. Over five thousand camps, mostly situated in the country, keep going three hundred thousand young people between the ages of seventeen and twenty-five. Many of them put in no more than half a year of work-service, and are then free to take employment elsewhere. They go forth, furnished with certificates, often to places awaiting them. Very possibly this volunteer service will develop later into an obligation. Plans are already in course of construction whereby such an army of workers can be employed for twenty years. The produce so raised will value two milliards of marks a year, and at least five thousand new peasant homesteads will be created.

Naturally the work done in these camps is of a supplementary order and is not allowed to compete in the open market with work turned out under ordinary conditions outside. Nor is such work undertaken which could as well be performed by private enterprise. It is the aim and object of these camps to promote facilities for other people, i.e. by the reclamation or improvement of waste land upon which settlements can be founded. The making of new roads, of course, opened up new ground for such a purpose. The settlement building itself is never undertaken by camp workers. The latter confine themselves to forestry, projects of land reclamation from the sea, canals, irrigation and particularly all undertakings which have for their aim the prevention of catastrophic happenings, forest fires, burst dykes, floods and so forth.

All this has proved of great practical utility. The young people in the Work Camps are well trained in the use of their various tools and implements, spades, pikes, shovels, etc., and can be quickly mustered and detailed for a job. Once on the occasion of a huge landslide on the Saale (a river in Central Germany), a serious disaster was only averted by the immediate mobilisation of young navvies from the nearest Work Camp, who immediately set to work to set things to rights. Many a village has been saved from extinction by fire by the exertions of such organised workers, and immense consequent misery avoided.

The campers themselves are willing and devoted enough. Each

man knows that his work benefits the community at large, and that he is therefore carrying out the fundamental principles of National Socialism. Hitler's worthy pronouncement, "There is only one nobility, the nobility of work," sustains these labourers through the heat and the toil of the longest day.

Life in a Labour Camp is not in the least modeled on the military plan. The workers rise at five in the summer, and at six in winter. Half an hour's exercise or sport precedes tubbing and breakfast. Then comes parade and the hoisting of the camp flag for the day. This resembles the Hooked Cross Flag only instead of the hooked cross in the white circle it displays a spade and a couple of ears of wheat. The whole is symbolic and recalls Frederick the Great's fine saying: "He who toils to make two ears of wheat grow where there was only one before, does more for his country than a general who wins a redoubtable victory."

After this parade the workers betake themselves to their various employments; the volunteers down tools at the end of a seven-hours' spell. Then comes a wash, and the midday meal eaten, naturally, in common. The food is good and everyone can have as much as he requires. An hour and half's "knock-off" ensues. The afternoon is taken up by a couple of hours of sport, and an hour's instruction in civics. The evening is passed in singing songs, and in reading aloud, etc., etc. Two or three evenings a week each man can call his own up to ten o'clock. Tattoo is at ten: everyone must then be in quarters.

The Work Camp brings all classes together. The student is set just the same jobs as any one else. The hope is that thirty years hence there will be no more intellectuals, or officials in Germany who have not passed through the school of manual work side by side with the everyday workman.

> Vergeßt nie, daß das heiligſte
> Recht auf dieſer Welt das Recht
> auf Erde iſt, die man bebauen will,
> und das heiligſte Opfer das Blut,
> das man für dieſe Erde vergießt
>
> Adolf Hitler

WHAT THE SOCIALISM REALLY MEANS

I t is scarcely necessary to enlarge, here, upon the "Nationalism" in Adolf Hitler's political creed. Enough has already been written about it. It has occupied so much space in the contemporary press and been discussed in so many books it has come to be regarded with a certain degree of Chauvinism. I propose, therefore, to confine myself, in the conclusion of this work to a few observations under the second heading of our double-barreled title. It is so completely true that he who studies contemporary Germany with a view to forecasting the future of the country must study it from inside and not from the outsider's point of view.[1] From outside one mainly perceives the nationalism. From the inside the drive and force of the socialism is most apparent.

German Socialism—Adolf Hitler's Socialism—is a totally dif-

1. This observation holds particularly good with regard to events in Germany since June 30th, 1934. Germany's political development has been along lines totally different from those in England and America, and has led to a type of political public opinion very different from that of the average Englishman or American. The latters make a great mistake to judge of affairs in another country as if they had happened in their own. This is the universal mistake of the onlooker and critics: perhaps it accounts for two-thirds of the international misunderstanding in Europe today.

---

ferent thing from what is generally understood by this term, from the Socialism derived from Marxian and Communistic theory. The first essential difference between the two consists in this, that the former is strictly national in aim, scope and limit; the latter is international, without boundaries of race or land. The second vital distinction is that the first has been set up by the wish of the people concerned, the second is imposed upon nations by the will of those who organise and propagate it. A third contrast can be drawn inasmuch as German Socialism tends to draw all sections of the nation closely together, international socialism initiates class war. German Socialism is directed by the country's nationals; International Socialism is an instrument of the Jews.[2] In the former it is the personality of the Leader wich tells; in the latter we have nothing but the inertia of the mass which is exploited by its organisers.

By the above signs is German Socialism to be recognised and distinguished. When it has completely assimilated Germany to itself, it will extend and become the groundwork for the future development of other countries. Marxism and Communism are finished in Germany. They have played their part and their rôle is over. Long enough have they made their influence felt in every sphere of German life, intellectual, political and economic, to the suppression of the truer socialism. Socialism is not a thing to be apprehended through dreary theory only, but to be tested and proved in action. We have written enough, elsewhere, very fully to show that the present German Government is inspired in its legislation by the spirit of active philanthropy which it calls Socialism. This legislation incorporates the very essence of German Socialism.

As Dr. Goebbels writes: "Socialism, as we understand it, does not reduce men to a dead level, but ranges them in order according to their individual capacity and leading. If I were to try and put our aims and objects in this direction in a nutshell, I should say that it is our endeavour to build up in Germany a people who all possess the same rights in life. We want everyone, high and low, to belong to such a people. We desire that the highest among them shall feel

2. *Vide* the period of the Soldiers' and Workmen's Councils in Munich.

themselves more closely united with the last and lowest of their own kith and kin than with the highest of any other nation. We aim at this — that the highest of our people would rather be the lowest of his own nation, than the highest of any other nation. Such an inspiration can only be the outcome of an absolutely unified national will."

It would lead too far afield to instance the many measures in which Hitler has exemplified his conception of true Socialism. We must confine ourselves to a mere sketch of the most important and obvious incorporations of the ideas through which he has restored to the German worker his honour and self-respect.

THE GERMAN LABOUR FRONT

The law of April 10th, 1933, which arranged May 1st as a great Labour Day Holiday initiated the above-named reorganisation of labour in Germany. The first celebration of the new holiday was unanimous and universal: the Germans had never had anything like it before. Thousands of people gathered together at the same time, all over the country, to listen to the Leader's speech, and then to make high holiday. All trades and callings and professions for the first time were assembled in common, symbolising the unity which was henceforth to unite both types of labour — that of the head, and that of the hand, symbolising the necessary equal value to the community of both. German Socialism recognises no discriminating difference between the brain worker and the hand worker.

Quick on the heels of May 1st and its celebrations came action. The German Labour Front emerged. On May 2nd the premises of all Marxian Labour Unions were taken over and the contents sequestered.

Abroad, similar Marxist Unions described this action of Hitler's as a theft of the German workman's hardly earned pay, saved up for years and years in the Unions' funds. Such a charge could not be substantiated, since these moneys were not taken from the workmen, to whom they rightly belonged, but from the greedy grasp of union officials to whom they did *not* belong, but who administered them wastefully, or appropriated them in disproportionate salaries.

With the workman himself went his money also, into the Labour Front. Here it could only be put to the best and most legitimate uses on his behalf.

The great object of the Labour Front is to secure German industry from the incessant recurrence of strikes and all their disintegrating consequences. German Socialism utterly opposes itself to strife between employers and men. Here again it shows quite a different face from that of Marxian Socialism which seeks to foment such discord, whereby, moreover, it maintains its own sovereignty.

In Germany today a strike is impossible for the reason that no employer dare pay less than the standardised daily wages, or the State would immediately take up the workers' grievance. On the other hand, were the workers to demand more than their due they themselves would bring about the collapse of the concern for which they worked. The standard of wages is arrived at by experts representing the men and concerned to secure their best interests.

Together with wages, the question of hours has also been considered. In Marxist-Socialist Germany after the War, very hard times set in for German working men. Their leaders had every opportunity to show what the theory could accomplish; they had a majority in the Reichstag, a member of the Party was President of the Reich. Nevertheless, they were all either too lazy or too indifferent to carry out their programme.

So long as the masses went hungry they were easy to inflame, and to excite against capitalism and the wealthy. While six and a half million unemployed hung about the streets while their wives and children were starving, selfish employers exploited the wretched state of things just because they were paying the dole, forsooth! If a man grumbled he lost his job, hundreds were only waiting to pounce upon in his stead. If he sought the assistance of the Secretary of his Union hew drew another blank. What cared the employer for the Unions? Should a strike ensue all he had to do was close shop or factory as the case might be, and say, "All right. We'll see who can stick it out the longest, you or I."

Days or even weeks might go by, but the result was always the same. The men came back with hangdog mien, glad to work again at any cost! This is where the German working man had lost in his own eyes. It was from this sort of victimisation and wretchedness that Hitler designed to rescue him, and give him back his self-respect. Hitherto he had been the prey of vicious circumstances, the slave of an unscrupulous class.

All was altered in a twinkling when Adolf Hitler came to power. A cry of gratitude and relief went up from all ranks of German working men. The Brown Shirts were everywhere welcomed as they made their way into shop and factory and yard to enquire after the needs and circumstances of every employee in the place. Union secretaries were haled to account no less than unsocialistic-minded employers. The German Labour Front was out to accomplish what it promised.

With the exception of peasants and officials, who have their own organisations, the German Labour Front comprises workmen of all kinds, employees, employers and people working on their own account. Hitler is its patron, Dr. Ley is its Leader. The standards of wages are carefully regulated and observed by reliable workers themselves. The Reich is divided up, under this scheme, into Regions, these, in turn, into Districts, there into Circuits or Local Groups, and these latter again into Trade Communes, Cells and Blocks.

STRENGTH THROUGH JOY

Perforce of its iron will, its absolute refusal to compromise and its terrific onset, National Socialism wrenched itself suddenly into power. Long years before this happened its better ideas had attracted people away from those of the old system then in vogue, and so it is readily to be understood how, in March, 1933, the aforesaid old system simply collapsed.

The first and greatest duty before National Socialism lies in winning the German people back to a sense of nationality, and in impressing its own principles upon them. A State that is to endure for centuries ahead must be built upon the very foundations of organic life, upon blood and soil, nationality and home.

In order to replace one kind of State with another, and better one, it is not enough merely to do away with the former: the people themselves must be re-educated. In place of a system full of class enmity and distinctions and pride of place there is now a commonwealth. The new State, organically designed, is founded upon the principle "The common good before that of the individual."

Under National Socialism the culture of an entire people must not be indentified with any particular caste, class, or level: it must characterise and belong to the mass. Nor must æsthetic enjoyments be only for the few; they must be common to all. Just as the creation of a united working people has been confided to the German Labour Front, so is it the business of another organisation, that of "Strength through Joy" to make every member of the nation free of its cultural and artistic treasures and resources. The two endeavours are interrelated. By means of the latter every German working man can look to his free evening as a real opportunity for refreshment and "uplift"; money which had formerly gone merely in organising strikes can now be spent far more profitably and agreeably.

It is not the object of "Strength through Joy" to educate the people politically. Few want to attend classes in civics after a hard day's work. Its aim is rather to bring the people together on a broad basis of enlightenment, an effort in which they, too, of course, must concur.

The Director of "Strength through Joy" is also Dr. Ley. His work is comprised under many headings. It is one of his principal endeavours to open up to worker and unemployed alike all the best sources of entertainment, opera, theatre and concert hall. For the fact that a workman in any German city can obtain admission to the finest operas for practically a nominal sum is Hitler himself directly to be thanked. Hitler often starved, in the old days, in order to buy the meanest standing room in the house, to hear Wagner. Now that he is Chancellor, no working man in Germany need be out to such shifts to gratify his artistic longings.

This "Kulturamt" has opened to the people all sorts of intellectual resorts hitherto sacred to the upper ten. It is a mistake to suppose that only such appreciate the best. In Germany Wagner takes precedence, even with the poorest people, over nigger minstrelsy and jazz.

Even the working man's week-ends are provided for. Previously he went for a bit of a walk in the park perhaps on Sunday, or took a tram out of the suburbs to get a breath of air. If he were a single man he might spend the most part of his leisure in a Bier Hall, listening to the band. Although this sort of thing can still be observed, everywhere, nowadays the workman looks to the sort of week-end right away which previously could only be enjoyed by the better to do. For a couple of marks, to-day, he can go thirty miles out of the city, follow a personally conducted tour around some beauty spots, and enjoy a good meal into the bargain. When his holiday comes around, it is provided for lavishly as far as good things are concerned, at equally small cost.

Workmen from Munich can now envisage holidays by the North Sea with all sorts of trips and bathing fun thrown in. Those from Berlin can go to the Alps, do a bit of mountaineering and try what hotel life is like. These are dreams come true which for whole generations past must have ever remained unrealisable. All thanks to Adolf Hitler.

The section of this activity which deals with "Volkstum und Heimat" seeks to revive, for urban populations, the knowledge of and delight in old peasant and traditional customs, songs, dances, costumes. This sort of thing reawakens love of the country and their origins in people long divorced from the land. It bridges the gulf between the peasant and the townsman.

"Kraft durch Freude" ("Strength through Joy") looks also to sport to give the working man zest and change in exercise. It is Hitler's keenest desire to see the worker, particularly the youthful worker (Hitler's Germany is all being built for the future – the past must now look after itself, "let the dead bury the dead" –) made "crisis resisting." The young workman goes in for tennis and golf and every other vigorous game that's going.

Through the instrumentality of innumerable exhibitions it is sought to rouse the worker's pride in his own achievements, in his niche in society, in the part he plays in the whole. His craft is displayed before him in its entire interest, or beauty, or siginificance. Prizes and competitions abound. Each man becomes conscious of the part he takes in the whole, and discovers fresh pride in his trades and in himself.

Cheap classes are held for those who desire to advance in their particular calling, or to study more particularly the trade to which they belong, and for the acquisition of foreign languages. The best teachers are retained and the instruction is given in the buildings of the local University.

People are assisted to acquire their own dwelling-houses. Loans for this purpose can be repaid by instalments over a series of years. In this way it is hoped to promote a cheerful small villadom beyond the limits of the greater cities.

The department for propaganda aims at bringing all these activities and facilities before the people, to encourage them to make the utmost of them. Only so will they be bringing about the National Socialist State envisaged by Adolf Hitler. There are still more departments in this one Movement alone, but space forbids their description.

Much, indeed, has been written about the new Germany. In England and America so much attention has been directed to its political aspect, that these others have been neglected. Of that attention, moreover, by far the greater part is highly inimical, highly critical. Few outside Germany yet realise why Hitler is prepared *to go to all lengths* to save this new Germany from being torpedoed either from within or without. He saves it in his own way and from those he considers enemies, whether his action is understood abroad or not.

Let those disbelive who will, Adolf Hitler has done more for Germany since he came to power than any other statesman at any other time, and the wrecking of his work would not only spell the final ruin of Germany, but the ruin of Europe at large. It is not too much that a handful of would-be saboteurs should die, by summary justice, to save a nation-wide, world-wide welter of blood. It is only time which can be trusted to explain all, to vindicate all, to crown all, and to show the proper greatness of

Adolf Hitler.

Bauernspruch

Ein freier Mann, dem ein Schwert gehört
Und ein Stück Land mit Weib und Kind
Und Brüder, die gleichen Blutes sind,
Das ist wie ein Schwur, den die Erde schwört.

Wo aber der Sinn verlorengeht
Für Hof und Tat und das hohe Geschlecht,
Das ist wie ein Fluch, der im Weltbaum weht
Uralt, urewig und hart und gerecht.

Reinder Sommerburg

HITLER, GERMANY AND THE WORLD

In order to round out the picture of Hitler which it has been the attempt of these pages to depict, a few words remain to be said about his private life since 1919.

As has already been narrated, Hitler left barracks in the August of that year, and rented a modest lodging with humble people in the Thierschstrasse, Number 41.

It is interesting to have a look into this poor room where Hitler lived for ten years. A Herr Erlanger is the landlord of the house. He observes to-day: "I hadn't much to do with him myself as he wasn't directly a tenant of mine. His room was a sub-let. And since I am a Jew, I concerned myself as little as possible with the activities of my lodger and the National Socialists. I admit, I liked Hitler well enough. I often encountered him on the stairway and at the door—he was generally scribbling something in a notebook—when he would pass the time of day with me pleasantly enough.

"Often he had his dog with him, a lovely wolfhound. He never made me feel he regarded me differently from other people. He lodged here in my house from the autumn of 1919 to 1929. First he took a little back room, and then an equally small one in the front to serve as a sort of office and study. The back room in which he slept is only eight by fifteen feet. It is the coldest room in the house; there's a passage below it leading to the courtyard. Some lodgers who've rented it since got ill. Now we only use it as a lumber room; nobody will have it anymore.

"The only 'comfort' Hitler treated himself to when he was here, was a hand basin with cold water laid on. The room to the front was a bit bigger, but the small high-set window left much to be desired. It was very scantily furnished."

We have caught a glimpse of the rooms that were his home all these strenuous years in the Thierschstrasse, and now we must have a look at his unpretentious house on the Obersalzberg.

Obersalzberg is one of the slopes of the Bavarian Alps, above the Königsee, but below the grand, bare, snow-flecked summits of the highest mountains near Watzmann. It is a shaggedly pine-wooded region interspersed with wide stretches and spaces of open grass or meadowland threaded by white filaments of winding road. The whole is dotted over with the characteristic Bauernhöfe (peasant farms) of the country, looking much like the chalets of Switzerland with their flower-decked balconies, their green-shuttered windows above the white stonework of the ground floor.

A steep road leads up from Berchtesgaden to the Obersalzberg. Here Hitler and a few chosen intimates found refuge from the stress and strain of life during the time that preceded the disruption of the Party in November, 1923. They forgathered in one of these Obersalzberg farm houses, called the Platterhof, and there took counsel together, and enjoyed brief, but precious, snatches of rest and recreation.

One gets to Berchtesgaden from Munich by train in about three hours. But by motor car one can do the journey a little more quickly. Berchtesgaden is a little town near the Königsee. It does not lie directly on the lake because the mountains there come down so steeply to the water's edge no room remains for the town. The lower flanks of these mountains are covered with hanging pine forests, but the summits are bare rock, snow-clad and glacier-seamed in winter. The Obersalzberg is a single mountain in the neighbourhood of the Königsee (King's Lake). There are houses built upon it. Lower down the slope of the Salzberg lay a little house, also built in the Bavarian mountain style, called Haus Wachenfeld.

Here the Bavarian Mountains meet the Salzberg Alps; the frontier indeed between Germany and Austria runs athwart these rocky summits. The view from hence is magnificent. Deep down below lies the green valley in which Berchtesgaden nestles. Snow-clad peaks soar into the blue heavens all around; among them König Watzmann and his seven rocky offspring.

Hitler's house, Wachenfeld, here, is in no sense an official ministerial residence like Chequers in England. It is not even a "country seat." It is nothing more than a simple country house.

It consists of two storeys, the lower built of white stone, the upper of brown stained wood. A wooden balcony with flower-boxes all along the railing runs round the house outside the bedroom windows. The windows have green shutters with white bands; the grey shingled roof is secured against the storms of winter by rows of heavy stones laid upon it. A little belfry, thatched, like a bird shelter, adorn one end of the roof tree. The plateau surrounding the house is laid out for a car park and a garden. There are flower borders, a large green lawn with a wide rectangular path surrounding it, a rock garden, a telescope, garden furniture—gay chairs, tables, coloured sun umbrellas—and a flagstaff with the long red flag and its hooked cross in the central circle of white, hanging from it.

All within is as simple and as well-kept as without. The peasant note is stressed. To describe one of the rooms: the furniture, consisting of little but the table and a few chairs, is of local make, of painted wood. A wooden dado in grey-green panels with a single little bunch of country flowers painted on each, reaches half-way up the cream-washed walls. The window has a vallance, and simple curtains of figured cretonne hang straight at the sides. A wooden bench coloured like the dado amply furnished with variously and gaily covered pillow-shaped cushions runs round the room and forms a window-seat. There are one or two wall-hung engravings to be noted, a cupboard with large painted panels, topped with jugs in peasant ware, and the bright notes of here and there a tasteful plate set on the beading of the dado. Such is the Reichskanzler's sitting or diningroom in Haus Wachenfeld. His square bare table has gaily turned and painted legs, and stretchers for foot rest between. All is eminently homelike and simple. A great green tiled oven, surrounded by a bench, takes the place of the English open hearth. Huge rag rygs lie here and there about the floor.

It is this home which is presided over by the Führer's widowed sister, Frau Angela Raubal.

Haus Wachenfeld was built shortly before the War by a Hamburg merchant. Hitler discovered it long before he bought it. His thoughts turned to this spot and this house after the strains and stresses of Landsberg.

He rented it, and asked his sister to come and keep house there, so that he himself could come and go as circumstances might permit. Later on he purchased it outright, and was thankful to withdraw to its peace and privacy during the stressful time of the struggle of the Party.

Later ensued a period during which but the rarest moments of respite could be snatched at Haus Wachenfeld. During the last phases of his struggle for power in 1932 Adolf Hitler rarely was able to resort thither, alone or with chosen companions, for a few hours' relaxation or intensive counsel.

There Frau Angela Raubal directed a household explicitly for this purpose. After a simple but sufficient repast in which fresh milk, black bread, and some sort of cereal were the chief ingredient, the Führer and his friends liked to sit round the table, or around the stove, and in this informal fashion talk over the prospects and the problems of the *Kampf*.

Since his accession to the Chancellorship of the Reich, Hitler's little country place has had to be adapted somewhat to its owner's wider needs. Without losing anything of its unpretentiousness, a motor road approach to it has been constructed, and additional accommodation has been added after the Führer's own plans. It remains, however, much as it was originally, and ever awaits the coming of its master, guarded by three friends of his of whom he has none more loyal and faithful, the sheepdogs, Muck, Wolf and Blonda.

By the year 1929 when Hitler's Party had now become a nation-wide Movement, it was unsuitable that he should remain any longer in the Thierschstrasse, mainly for the reason that he was obliged to receive the visits of highly placed or important people either in his inadequate little room there, or in the back premises in the Schellingstrasse used as Party headquarters. So he removed to an empty apartment in the Prinzregenten Platz 16, "This bachelor requires nine rooms for himself," wrote one of his critics and opponents, quite failing to add that two families also shared them, one of these consisting of the very people with whom he had lodged in the Thierschstrasse.

Hitler still lives in this house when in Munich. His pretensions have waxed no whit since he became Chancellor.

He generally comes of a week-end to Munich or to Berchtesgaden. The rest of the time he spends in Berlin. He inhabits the old Reichskanzlei of Prince Bismarck. As a rule he takes his frugal meals at home, often in company with a few simple S.A. men who come to him from every quarter, some of whom he may not even know. His adjutant Brückner sees to it, doubtless, that it is not always the same visitors who have the privilege of dining with Adolf Hitler.

Personal comfort, apart from personal cleanliness, never meant much to Hitler. He lives as simply to-day in the Wilhelmstrasse as he lived at Frau Popp's and in the Thierschstrasse in those early beginnings.

He exacts the ideal of "the simple life" from his followers, although this is not the same thing as to say he would, generally, lower the standard of living. He would raise the standard of living, but *equalise* (socialise) it.

To-day the whole world demands "Whither Germany?" The answer is simple. One can only reply, "Germany follows Hitler." Who would predict the course the Fatherland will pursue should study the life of the Führer, mark its consistency from the beginning up to the present, and only so venture on prophecy. It is impossible to foretell what line his policy will take if he is only considered from the angle of politics and diplomacy. Hitler must be estimated from the human side as well.

Anyone who has so studied Hitler's career, especially that period of it in Vienna which preceded his taking up politics, will grant that he has not deviated from the views he formed as a young man either in respect of them or with regard to the conduct of life in general.

And, as has been so often remarked, place and power have not altered the manner of man he was.

So, like Hitler himself, the Party holds straight on its course, and with it, Germany. Hitler is no weathercock, to be twirled this way and that by every wind that blows. Other people's views cannot influence his decisions. He goes direct to his object, without detour. This object is none other than the accomplishment of the Party programme.

The onlookers at the Third Reich often believe they can detect a leaning in Hitler's policy to the "Right" or the "Left" of his Cabinet. The affair at Wiessee, the arrest of Röhm, gave enormous scope for this type of criticism. It overflowed the entire Press. The summary action of the Führer was ascribed most contradictorily either as a "swing to the left," or as one "to the right," according to the way the critics estimated his reaction to the situation and the forces behind it. As a matter of fact it was neither. Hitler went, as usual, straight ahead, straight to his one object—the stabilisation of the Third Reich.

The present writer, who was not only in Munich at the time of the Röhm scandal, but actually in the Brown House itself, had sufficient inside knowledge of the circumstances to affirm that had not Hitler acted with the promptitude and severity that he did, a hideous massacre would forthwith have taken place in the city. All was set for a violent clash between the S.A. Troops and the heavily armed Reichswehr. This piece of treachery was scotched, on the instant, before it could be realised.

But a great part of the non-German Press was loud in its outcry on behalf of the mutineers, stigmatising Hitler's action as that of a murderer. Only a short while previous to the painful events of June 30th no one of these newspapers could sufficiently condemn Röhm and his associates. To the man in the street in Germany the contradiction here is, to say the least of it, extraordinary. He can only conclude that Hitler will always be misrepresented so long as Truth herself suffers the same misfortune.

Germany's foreign policy is directed towards peace and good understanding. Foreign nations make a great mistake when they confuse National Socialism with Imperialism. National Socialism has no designs upon other lands and other peoples. Germany's future lies in its keeping, and, indeed, that of the whole world — in the keeping of the true Socialism of common life, not in that of class war.

Socialism as an international aspiration has practically petered out. It reached its apogee towards the end of the War, and at the moment when it made its bid for power, its failure began.

The future belongs to National Socialism since, like Christianity itself, it is founded on love, and reconiliation between high and low, rich and poor. Herein lies its special creative and effective power. Marxian Socialism, on the contrary, flourishes on class clash and hatred. It is anti-Christian and destructive.

The world will come to the recognition of all this in time. It may be decades will be required before the truth of the contention is established beyond cavil. Later generations will consider the Period

---

of Marxian Socialism as an interlude out of which purgatory the
world emerged into the truer and beneficent conception of

Adolf Hitler.

Hitler, the Workless and the Needy, What the Socialism Really Means, *and* Hitler,
Germany and the World *have been excerpted from* Germany's Hitler, *by Heinz A.
Heinz, originally published in 1934 by Hurst & Blackett, Ltd., London, and are available
as reprints from Liberty Bell Publications at the following prices:* Hitler, the
Workless and the Needy, *$1.50.* What the Socialism Really Means & Hitler, Germany
and the World, *$2.50. Please add $1.50 for orders under $10.00, 15% for
orders over $10.00 for postage and handling.*

Reichsjugendtag in Potsdam. 1932

NATIONAL SOCIALISM: THEN AND NOW

A Philosophical Appraisal

by *Colin Jordan*

FOREWORD

In this classic little exposé of the Philosophy of National Socialism, Colin Jordan, an Englishman, lays bare in a few well chosen paragraphs what alone can save mankind from total chaos and ultimate degeneracy and extinction.

Here the forces of light meet the powers of death and darkness—head on.

Every white home, every white student, every white parent, teacher, and businessman should be made available a copy of this booklet.

No greater gift could be made to members of our race then this little booklet at this crucial time. Widely distributed and circulated, it will pull back white men and women everywhere from the brink of self-destruction.

Here, captured in a few pages, the trailblazing thoughts of a German genius, Adolf Hitler, member of our race, are appraised by a brilliant mind, an English school teacher, who exposes and thus makes universally available the only key to a healthier and saner world. A new world where all races will live in natural harmony, where healthy upward-striving competition will result in a new kind of man — a new mankind.

National Socialism is not German — nor is it only for Whites — National Socialism means the new mankind.

He came as saviour to a stricken West
but the makers of ruin defeated him. Now their record proves
how right he was.
April 20, 1989
Honour the centenary of his birth, and show thereby
that his spirit lives and will triumph yet.
J.C.C. Jordan
Thorgarth, Greenhow Hill
Harrogate, N. Yorks. HG3 5JQ, England

NATIONAL SOCIALISM: THEN AND NOW

A Philosophical Appraisal

Several decades after the physical defeat of National Socialist Germany in the outcome of her heroic struggle against the overwhelming array of men and materials marshalled against her by the Bolshevistic-Democratic alliance, the appearance of this reappraisal reflects the revival of National Socialism which is the feature of the day.

That the creed should live on and manifest itself as it does now, after being subjected to decades of the greatest campaign of defamation which the world has ever known, is a proof of its continuing validity and appeal and its worthiness for the future. It has survived the flames of war and the tempest of vilification because, when war has done its worst and vilification runs its entire gamut, National Socialism remains, in the final analysis, synonymous with higher man's will to survive, his instinct for health and strength, his desire to remain on this earth, the creed of National Socialism will remain, indestructible.

Beyond and behind all the minutiae of political implementation and the particularities of time and place, National Socialism, properly understood, is nothing less than an orientation of the mind, the dominant impulse of which is to live to the full, through the development of one's potentialities and the satisfaction of one's needs, under conditions of natural competition and selection, reconciled to coöperation, within the organized community of the folk.

In this its roots go back to Plato's Greece and his conception of a natural life, consisting in the full realization of man's true nature through the conducive power of government within his native community.

It echoes the Roman notion of dutiful citizenship: the notion that the good and noble life consists in stoic service to the state.

It revives the blood feelings and sense of community of the Nordic tribes of early Europe: the feeling that man is essentially a member of the folk, and that all members of the folk are bound together closely with reciprocal duties and obligations.

National Socialism, in this way, reaches back to the old, healthy, organic values of life in revolt against the whole structure of thought of liberalism and democracy, with its cash nexus; its excessive individualism; its view of man as a folkless, interchangeable unit of world population; its spiritual justification in a debased Christianity embracing a sickly "humanitarianism," which will always tolerate a greater harm for the sake of avoiding a lesser one; and its fraudulent contention that the artificially induced and numerically determined wishes of the mass are the all-important criteria.

History is a saga of social decay and renewal. National Socialism is the twentieth century's remedy of renewal for the great degeneration of modern times under the disintegrating, debasing, and emasculating thought and practice which emerged with the disruption of the old medieval order of stability by the developing forces of capitalism and the industrial revolution; flourished under the laissez-faire liberalism of the eighteenth and nineteenth centuries; came to a climax under the democracy of the nineteenth and twentieth centuries; and will result in the world triumph of Communism by the end of this twentieth century unless National Socialism comes to power in time, over a sufficient area of the globe.

National Socialism, therefore, is immensely more than a transitory political scheme. It is an historic tendency of rebirth: our age's movement of renaissance, a movement revolutionary in scope and spirit, seeking no compromise with the present order, its pernicious practices, and its false values, but their complete replacement.

As such it is worldwide in that, in its essentials, it is valid and vital universally, qualified only by the fact that it is Aryan in emanation and tradition, and upholds and depends on qualities to be found *par excellence* in the Aryan people.

It is life-wide in that it is not an *aspect* of life, but the whole of life seen from one aspect. It is an attitude of mind expressible in respect of virtually anything and everything. National Socialism stands relentlessly opposed to every manifestation of ill health, ugliness, and degeneracy in the cultural and spiritual, no less than in the political and economic spheres. In fact, it constitutes a way of life. A man does not call himself a National Socialist as a mere label of intellectual endorsement. He is born with a propensity to National Socialism, his mind aesthetically craving the discernment and fulfillment of a healthy pattern of life, and he not only thinks and feels, but *acts* as a National Socialist, if he is really and entirely one.

Total in its scope of thought, National Socialism amounts to a philosophy and a faith. It evaluates good and bad, right and wrong, as that which benefits or harms the folk, and man viewed as a member of the folk; and, in place of the sentimental debility of the democratic mind, accepts that the end justifies the means, providing the means do not contradict the end. It sets a meaning and purpose of cosmic dimension to life as a personal fulfillment, within the continuity and development of the folk, between germination in the womb out of the bloodline of the folk, and the metamorphosis of the grave, with its physical redistribution to the universe.

The basic criterion and primary value of National Socialism, from which all else springs, is, as Adolf Hitler makes clear in *Mein Kampf*, its concept of the folk, seen as man's essential environment and, indeed, his extension of personality.

The significance of the folk is, primarily that of a racial community. It is the ethnical enlargement of the family. Man is not a self-contained unit and an end in himself, as the sages of liberalism and democracy assert. He belongs to his folk. His life, as a part, is interwoven with the life of the whole, not only present, but past and future, for while men come and go the folk lives on, continuous, eternal, providing its members perform their duty to it. Thus, in identifying himself with his folk, man prolongs himself through the multiplicity of his ancestors and his descendants, and thereby attains immortality.

The folk exists in smaller and larger forms, ranging from the family, to the clan, to the tribe or regional community, thence to the nation, and beyond to the race. In modern times, the conception of the folk has become too largely identified with the nations of the contemporary states. The feeling of kinship and community, which rightly expanded from the tribe and petty kingdom to the modern nation-state, has, however, become far too concentrated at this level. The lower and smaller, but equally important, communities within the nation-state have been disrupted and deprived of vitality, while the expansion of folk consciousness from the level of the nation-state to that of the entire race has been checked. Yet folk feeling, to be wholesomely potent, must flow from its roots through the local and provincial communities to the limits of the race, because the full security and prosperity of the parts can only be found in that of the whole.

Today and in the future National Socialism must embody this essential extension of the feeling of kinship and community beyond the bounds of the contemporary nation-state and conventional nationalism, so that the nation-state becomes an intermediate unit in the structure of the folk, and its nationalism and racialism becomes integrally subordinate to a nationalism of the whole race.

At the same time, the local communities require to be revived, the provincial sub-nations recognized and respected, and peoples subject to an undesired, alien rule given their ethnic freedom by separation.

National Socialism's belief in the folk as the basic value, and its totality of outlook, result, figuratively speaking, in *thinking with the blood* on all questions.

This immediately and inevitably gives rise to the definition of citizenship as a matter of race: only those who are members of the folk are members of the nation, and only those who are members of the nation can be citizens of the state—to paraphrase the fourth of Twenty-five Points of Adolf Hitler's NSDAP.

It also generates the belief that it is necessary not merely to preserve the racial character of the folk, but also, by eugenic measures, to improve the quality of the folk. It is National Socialism's revolutionary contention that the way of real progress lies in breeding better human beings.

Since all citizens are of the same race, they have a transcendent bond of kinship uniting them as blood brothers above all sectional and class differences and personal distinctions. National unity, i.e., cohesion and corporate life in place of the class warfare of Left and Right, is one of the great secondary principles of National Socialism. All occupations, and pursuits, all manner of persons and all fields of activity, must be integrated into the corporate life of the community.

The social feeling of oneness must find practical expression in, and in turn be stimulated by, a sincere and profound concern for social and economic justice. Consciousness of kinship and care for the collective good of the folk demand that every citizen must have an equal opportunity to develop and exercise his talents and rise according to his merits; and that every citizen must receive a fair return for his services to the community, and even the simplest worker an assurance of the necessities of life.

Thus we arrive at the socialist element in National Socialism. This is not the Marxist socialism of state ownership of the means of production and distribution, which is the economic over-government of the ant-heap, and as objectionable as the predatory individualism of the capitalist system, which is the economic under-government, or anarchy, of the jungle. Instead it is Folk Socialism, or the regulation of private enterprise for the equitable division of its fruits, under equitable conditions. The economic injustices and social evils of capitalism have fostered Marxism, with its pernicious form of public control of the economy, and the alternative to both lies in National Socialism.

The folk ideal, which entails the defense of the race, the unity of the nation, and the welfare of the people, engenders National Socialism's principle of leadership and an élite in the service of those objectives. Its conception of a natural order is one which not only ordains that men are born into the folk for a life within the folk, but also that they possess hereditary differences of capacity to serve the community.

Accordingly, for the maximum good of all, the superior must lead the inferior. The natural leaders must be selected, established as a hierarchic élite under a supreme leader, and empowered to fulfil their functions.

Unlike liberalism, National Socialism does not regard the directive power of the state as something essentially repressive, but instead as a great, beneficial power of guidance and arbitration, encouragement and protection. It upholds the dictum: "All for the folk and folk for all." It sanctions whatever means are necessary, in whatever fields, to ensure that everyone and everything in the community is in harmony with this.

It sees the duty of National Socialist government as the representation of the will of the folk, conceived not as the transitory whim of some democratic mob, but as the higher interest of the community, viewed in historical perspective as a continuity of purpose, embracing not only the general good of the present, but the heritage of the past and the needs of the future as well.

Reprinted with permission from: *National Socialist World*

WAS ENDLICH DOCH SIEGEN WIRD,
IST DAS FEUER DER DEUTSCHEN
JUGEND.   *ADOLF HITLER*

TO ARYAN YOUTH
by
Dr. Walter Gross

Aryans are those non-Jewish White persons, wherever they may reside in the world today, who share substantially in the genetic heritage left us by those great forebears who, emerging in wave after wave from their northern European heartland throughout the millennia, conquered and organized the known world; and who created the great civilizations of Greece and Rome, as well as that of the West after the classical civilizations had disintegrated under the influence of racial mixture and decay. . .

Preface

The following is the translation of a short address which appeared in the December, 1935, issue of *Neues Volk*, the official publication of the Racial-political Department of the NSDAP. Dr. Walter Gross (Ph.D., Heidelberg, 1934), head of the Department, is the author of numerous books and articles on racial matters.

More than any other single aspect of the National Socialist ideology, the racial aspect has been deliberately misrepresented and distorted by the Jewish-democratic world press for the purpose of fomenting hatred against National Socialists and their beliefs. This brief address gives us a glimpse at the doctrine, as presented in Germany, which was and still is hysterically characterized as "preposterous," "virulent," "appallingly crude," "demented," and "sadistic."[1] We leave it to the reader to judge who is demented.

When we speak today about race and blood, we touch upon a subject which stands at the focus of the intellectual and philosophical struggles of our times. You know, of course, that all the political and spiritual opponents of our movement have in the course of time had to admit that we are right in the fields of politics and economics, and today they can't get around admitting the accomplishments of National Socialism, however unwilling they are to do so. But as soon as the talk turns to the spiritual foundations of National Socialism, as soon as the idea upon which we base everything comes into question, objections arise. Now as ever, it is the racial ideas of National Socialism whose justification is doubted or even bluntly disputed. A glance in the foreign press will show us that; and we find it in discussions all the time with groups in our own country who feel even now that they cannot accept certain parts of the National Socialist philosophy.

I have already talked about what we mean by racial thinking in the most general sense, and have pointed out with emphasis that for us the teaching of blood and race does not mean primarily an important and interesting bit of biological science, but above all a political and philosophical principle which basically determines our attitude on many questions of life. The two most important facts which form the basis for this principle are knowledge of the powers of hereditary transmission and a recognition of the deep, even spiritual meaning of the racial differences within mankind. Because we are aware of dependence upon hereditary abilities and talents,

1. All these descriptions are applied by William L. Shirer in his all-too-well-known book, *The Rise and Fall of the Third Reich* (New York, 1959).

we do not fall into the old error of overestimating educational measures and the effects of care and training; we are conscious of our responsibility to pass on our own heredity because only from it flows strength for the future. We are modest about every achievement of our own, for it has its roots in the abilities which we have received from our forebears without any doing on our part; and at the same time we're proud to see ourselves and our own short lives as links in the chain of generations and to feel that we are the bridge which leads from a great past into the most distant future.

And because we have learned, on the other hand, to recognize and respect the physical and spiritual individuality of the various human races, we have gotten away from the sickly ambition of striving for an indiscriminate "equalization" and a barren sameness in the areas of politics, economics, culture, and religion. We have recognized again the characteristics of our own race and wish to foster and preserve them, because they are a God-given form in which we live our lives as a nation and a people. At the same time we've gotten a better appreciation of the traits of this world's other races to the extent that we are no longer so anxious to make them follow our ways of thinking and feeling at any price, but we are convinced that they too can live and deal only according to the laws of their own nature.

That is about the content of racial thinking as we teach and learn it. And now when we ask ourselves why there is so much quarreling over such a simple and yet great idea, we find with closer examination that the reasons for the reaction have changed in many ways in the course of time. The opponents of our racial theories have remained firm in rejecting the new ideas, but they have repeatedly changed the grounds that they stand on themselves, and have forced us in the process to continually open and present these questions from a new position.

In the beginning, years ago, in other words, when people first dared to speak of race in this rotten age of liberal-bourgeois thinking and Marxist corruption, they attacked the dangerous new ideas sharply on so-called scientific grounds. Some critics simply challenged the correctness of our biological findings. Armchair experts ridiculed racial knowledge and its teachers, and from lecterns, in editing rooms, and in meeting halls they tried to make it seem that they were dealing with only a handful of amusing fools and their wild imaginations. It is a good idea to look back today on that time and bring to mind once more the underhanded tactics of our ideology's foes. There were serious, experienced scientists even then who worked out the foundations of a completely new conception of things, while the opposition used all possible means of discrediting and slandering them, keeping up this barrage for years on end. The much-vaunted scientific freedom was trampled under foot because that suited the ruling powers of the time.

Now we have that part of the fight happily behind us.[2] Today it is clear to men in all camps and all countries of the world that one cannot seriously doubt the scientific and biological basis of our racial views, and all truly scientific discussions on this subject have for some time been devoted only to broadening our knowledge in individual areas, and the actual correctness of the basic ideas is no longer questioned. So things have quieted down in the world of science; the enemies of our beliefs have had to take up new positions in order to defend their old values against the modern age. They soon found a new slogan for the fight; "in the name of humanity and morality" people prepared to combat a view whose scientific merit could no longer be contested, but whose effects in national life might nevertheless be unbearable and even disastrous. You know what kind of accusations have come up in the course of months; for example, the theory of heredity is supposed to be dangerous because it relieves man of the responsibility for his own life and always gives him a chance to excuse his laziness, baseness, and weakness of character as inherited tendencies. Worried old maids

2. Unfortunately, this is not yet so. Dr. Gross did not reckon with the incredible arrogance of a loud and influential group of American-Jewish pseudo-anthropologists who still today noisily maintain that there really are no such things as distinct races and no evidence at all that there exist hereditary psychic or intellectual differences between the races.

of both sexes wrung their hands and watched an age of immorality and shamelessness roll in which they felt must be blamed on that false doctrine, the National Socialist race theory. We joined in the battle too, and may well say that we have already won it. For when such objections to our views are raised, it is really nothing more than a sly evasion of the facts.

Certainly we are not masters of our destinies, because we are always dependent upon the form which we inherit, and that is determined by heaven. But that certainly doesn't mean that nothing more can be done with us, or other people, for that matter. On the contrary, what we do with our inherited talents for the good or bad depends entirely upon us; we can let our abilities be wasted and misused, or we can train and develop them. We can lazily let our bad or useless traits grow more dominant or we can fight courageously all our lives to overcome them. This is a decision that each person has to make (and which society demands of everyone), so we place the great, difficult precept of individual responsibility next to knowledge of the hereditary determination of our characters.

This is a clear, understandable principle; even our enemies have gradually calmed down when faced with it. Today they must grudgingly admit the moral correctness of our interpretation, just as they had to credit our scientific accuracy. So now they are leaving also the second position in their running fight. But already there is a new battle beginning in a new and, frankly speaking, more important area. Now the objection arises that while the National Socialist racial theory may be completely correct and may also be educationally and morally sound, it must nevertheless be rejected in the name of faith, religion, and piety. It is said that we are on the point of putting blood in the place of God as a sort of idol, thereby replacing the human soul with a man-made theory, or at best with body and matter.

If we ask ourselves about the reasons why people always try to disturb the ideological unity of the German people on religious grounds, we come up with this very same reproach again and again, though with a thousand variations. It constitutes the last opposition to the victorious idea of our movement.

Dear boys and girls! We want to face these outmoded bogeymen again in this third round of the great struggle of the present day with our accustomed boldness and vigor. And with perfect reason, because no accusation can be more dishonest or stupider than the one we've just discussed. Nobody really has any idea of advocating empty materialism in connection with our racial teachings. Certainly nobody wants to turn the admitted fact of race into any kind of idol and to destroy real religious feeling with it. But we believe in any case that we have the right to demand more attention and respect for our racial views, just as the obviously irreligious and overbearing philosophies of the past have been able to do. If we bow again before the facts of creation instead of trying to argue them away with liberal or scholastic squabbling, is that somehow supposed to be anti-religious? If we recognize once more the way in which our own nature is regulated by hereditary characteristics dictated by the Almighty, do you call that human conceit and idolatry? If we humbly admit that as human beings we are bound by race and cannot do otherwise than to think, feel, and act according to the ways which our blood demands and which God himself has established in us, is that heresy and disbelief, or isn't it rather a bit of piety in the truest sense of the word? Yes indeed, in the facts and precepts of race, we see something sacred and holy. This is not because we want to build up our own egos, but because we, being more honest than our opponents, recognize and admit the power of the Creator. This is something that has been very inconvenient for many political systems of the past. When we try to maintain the differences and special merits of the various races which heaven created, we thereby serve the Creator and obey His laws, and so act in better faith than the quarreling scholars who value their dull, ashen dogmas above the facts of real life. If the best men of all times and peoples have drawn the deepest, truest religious feeling from a look at the world's great order and nature, we acknowledge proudly yet humbly that to us the laws of blood and race, with their wonderful interrelationship and difficult demands, form a holy part of that great order in which we recognize the Almighty.

And so once again we raise the banner of Life against every doctrine of weakness and death, and we prepare for the future with a confession of faith: our blood is sacred to us as the thing that forms us in the image of God.

Reprinted from the Fall, 1966, issue of *National Socialist World*,
©1969 by William L. Pierce.

THE MOST ANCIENT
SWASTIKA EVER FOUND IN EUROPE

Nur einer war, der vorwärts schritt,
als brach und tot die Äcker lagen!

Nur einer war, der für uns stritt -
er warf die Saat, ein Volk ging mit
und wollte stolz die Zukunft tragen!

Und aus den Herzen wuchs der Sieg
des Glaubens, dem er sich verschworen! -
Als eine ganze Welt in Krieg
und Not und Elend abwärts stieg,
hat ihn das Schicksal uns erkoren!

Nun liegt das Schwert mit starker Kraft
befreiend über diesem Werke.
Was der Triumph des Willens schafft,
wird nimmermehr hinweggerafft!
In Ehre steht ein Volk der Stärke!

Es rinnt die Zeit. - Das Saatkorn reift.
Bald wird der Schnitter sich bereiten - -
Wenn seine Faust die Sense greift
und blitzend durch die Halme streicht,
wird stolz dies Volk zur Ernte schreiten!

Hein Meiswinkel

Bekenntnis

Ich, einer von den Letzten und den Alten,
Will treu zu dir, der einst uns führte, halten.
Und sind auch deine Fehler offenbar:
Zu allem stehe ich, was einstens war.

Bei deiner Asche schwör ich, großer Mann:
In Treue stand ich, als der Kampf begann.
Du hast mir selber einst die Hand gedrückt
Und mich mit blauen Augen angeblickt.

Nun, da das Heil'ge Reich versunken ist
Und du nicht mehr auf dieser Erde bist,
Steh ich, gealtert und in weißem Haar,
Für alles ein, was einst uns teuer war.

Ich bleibe unsern hehren Zielen treu.
Mein letzter Stolz ist: Ich war auch dabei!

Meine Ehre heißt Treue!

Deutschland, wie lieb ich dich, Land meiner Ahnen,
Dir sei mein ganzes Leben geweiht.
Unter der Treuesten ruhmreichen Fahnen
Gelte nur dir mein heiliger Eid.
Aus meines Herzens tiefstem Grunde
Mein Gelöbnis ich täglich erneue:
      Meine Ehre heißt Treue!

Deutschland, dir, wie einst die Väter dich schufen,
Aus zerrissenen Stämmen ein stolzes Reich.
Wehrtest den Stürmen auf schnellen Hufen,
Bollwerk des Abendlandes zugleich.
Dir, Deutschland, gilt aus meinem Munde
Mein heiliger Schwur stets aufs neue:
      Meine Ehre heißt Treue!

Aber den Welten steht richtend der Höchste,
Der in uns die Stimme des Blutes entfacht.
Ich bin mir bewußt, der wäre der Nächste,
Den träfe die Schande, des Volkes Acht,
Der, wollt' er die Stimme verletzen.
Zu spät käme nachher die Reue. —
      Meine Ehre heißt Treue!

Alles was dräuend erhebt sich im Leben,
Zerschellen soll es an meiner Treu'.
Für Deutschland bin ich bereit alles zu geben,
Taten für Deutschland ich niemals bereu',
Mag sich der Gegner entsetzen.
Dir, Deutschland, gilt ewig aufs neue:
      Meine Ehre heißt Treue!

Bremen, den 6. August 1959   Hans Hermann Weler

Deutſch ſein heißt:

Treu ſein –
Wahr ſein –
Kämpfer ſein.

Und Kämpfer ſollt ihr ſein,
Kämpfer für alles Gute und Schöne.

Dazu Heil!   Horſt Weſſel

www.ingramcontent.com/pod-product-compliance
Lightning Source LLC
Chambersburg PA
CBHW022113280326
41933CB00007B/369